Complete Guide to
PROFITABLE REAL ESTATE LEASING

Complete Guide to PROFITABLE REAL ESTATE LEASING

DAVIS T. BOHON

Prentice-Hall, Inc.

Englewood Cliffs, N. J.

PRENTICE-HALL INTERNATIONAL, INC., *London*
PRENTICE-HALL OF AUSTRALIA, PTY. LTD., *Sydney*
PRENTICE-HALL OF CANADA, LTD., *Toronto*
PRENTICE-HALL OF INDIA PRIVATE LTD., *New Delhi*
PRENTICE-HALL OF JAPAN, INC., *Tokyo*

LIBRARY OF CONGRESS
CATALOG CARD NUMBER: 69-13298

PRINTED IN THE UNITED STATES OF AMERICA

13-160333-7 B & P

A Word from the Author

One of the rewarding fields that many real estate owners, investors and brokers overlook is that of making leases. Most brokers seem to think entirely in terms of the sale of real estate and do not think about the advantages of leasing it. Frequently the commission on a good lease exceeds that of a good sale. The commission on a long-term lease on commercial property can sometimes exceed the commission that would be earned on a two or three hundred thousand dollar outright sale.

Leasing is big business with all types of real estate. More people tend to live in rented property rather than own their home outright. This is especially true of apartment houses. In recent years, there have been an untold number of apartment houses built, nearly all of which are occupied. The same is true of duplexes, resort type property and even of single family homes. It is especially true in commercial property that many owners do not want to sell, but prefer to make a land lease or build improvements to suit good tenants and lease to them. On the other side of the picture, many concerns who are in the manufacturing or wholesale or retail business are not interested in investing in real estate, but prefer to keep their capital in the active operation of the business. For this reason, they are much more interested in leasing property than in purchasing it. This observation is true of industrial firms, wholesale firms and all kinds of stores. The tremendous development of shopping centers almost invariably is a matter of an investor building a shopping center and leasing it to good tenants. Service stations are very active in leasing property, frequently leasing the land, putting their own improvements on it or getting the land owner to build to their specifications and leasing to them. There has also been an enormous expansion of the amount of office space, with many new office buildings, many older ones remodeled and a number enlarged to furnish extra space. The demand for office space is very large on the part of service concerns like insurance companies, finance companies, and so forth. The leasing of office space can contribute to the profits of any investor or broker. The matter of leasing even extends to agricultural land, as many farms are leased to tenants who do the actual work of operating the farm. It is also true of hotels and motels, which are frequently constructed by investors who in turn lease them to operating companies. In general, there is hardly any phase of real estate that does not intimately involve leasing.

The importance of leasing to the broker or to any investor is easy to see when it is realized how vast the leasing business is and how much money is involved. On a long-term lease of fifteen years, for example, to a commercial firm where the lease may run as high as one hundred thousand dollars per year, the amount of rental money paid over the term of the lease is one million five hundred thousand dollars. Since most commission schedules are based on the entire rent paid over the period of the lease, it is obvious leasing is very lucrative indeed for the broker. Sometimes the commission is paid all at one time at the time the lease is made, and sometimes it is paid over the period of the lease as the rent is paid. Leasing is even more important to the owner of the property, since a properly negotiated lease produces a fine income for many years.

Actually, about the only way a real estate broker can obtain a steady and reliable income for himself is through commissions on long-term leases. On a fifteen- or twenty-year lease where the commission is paid over the period of the lease, the broker is assured of a regular income for that time. As he makes other leases, the cumulative effect of this income can be very substantial. If he makes a lease every three or four months, in a few years, the income from these leases will be very profitable. If this book can help brokers learn how to obtain sizable commissions from leasing real estate, and help property owners obtain greater incomes, it will have accomplished its purpose.

While this book was in preparation, I have had occasion to call upon many individuals for information and advice. I would like to take this opportunity to convey my special thanks to: Miller Welch, Realtor, Lexington, Kentucky; David M. Trapp, Owner, Gardenside Plaza Shopping Center, Lexington, Kentucky; Senator William L. Sullivan, Owner, Old Orchard Shopping Center, Henderson, Kentucky; and Holmes F. Coats, Realtor, Lexington, Kentucky.

Contents

Exhibits

Chapter 1

How to Make Money Giving Prospective Tenants What They Want

If you are going to be successful in effecting leases, the first thing to keep in mind is that you should have property for lease that is attractive and is suitable for tenants. All prospective tenants are different, and each one has his own needs and ideas as to what he wants to lease. However, there are certain general considerations applicable to most types of tenants which you can use as rules in evaluating the value of rental property. Before undertaking to lease property of any kind, you should determine how attractive the particular property will appear to prospective tenants. Some properties are much easier to lease than others, and since you want properties that will lease more quickly and easily, you must offer those that are most suitable for tenants.

LOCATION

Probably the one aspect that most affects the desirability of property which is offered for rent is its location. This is important in all types of property.

Residential Property

Any type of residential property (single family homes, duplexes, or apartments) is especially attractive if it is in a good neighborhood with good surroundings, and if it is near schools, churches and shopping centers. In this matter of location, the single most important consideration is, of course, the character of the neighborhood. Is it in an area where the homes are neat and attractive or in one that is obviously run-down? A quick ride around the neighborhood will soon tell you whether or not it would be attractive for homes. If it is a run-down neighborhood, the rent will probably be lower. Consequently, you may still be able to lease it, but it is a more difficult job, the commission is less, and you will not come out as well from a remuneration standpoint.

Another important point concerning location is its accessibility. Is it on a good street by which it is easy to reach areas to which the home owner frequently goes, such as shopping centers, schools, churches and places of amusement (neighborhood theaters, etc.)? It is also very helpful if the property is located not far from a golf course. There is some advantage if the property is located on a street with easy access to a bypass road or an interstate road. With as much traveling as the average family does today, this is a distinct advantage to most people.

Commercial Properties

While the matter of location is important to residential tenants, it is of far greater significance to commercial tenants. Businesses must be located in areas in which they may be operated with the maximum of efficiency. The type of location varies with the type of business; but in all of them, it is extremely important. Factories and concerns of an industrial character, such as warehouses, must be located near interstate highways. Sometimes, if the particular industry uses freight shipments to any extent, it should be located on a rail line with the appropriate siding. Offices must be located in such a way that they can be easily accessible to customers or clients that call at the office. They should also be located in such a way that it is convenient for the employees to reach them. In recent years, there has been a tendency to construct office buildings in outlying sections of the city, and this seems to work all right provided there are good roads, preferably main highways or expressways, leading to them.

Wholesale businesses generally must be located where it is easy for trucks to reach and should be close to major highways.

The requirements of retail businesses vary a great deal according to the type of business. The service station specializes, of course, in automobile traffic and usually should be on a corner, so as to attract traffic from two streets. There are other types of retail businesses that are primarily interested in pedestrian traffic. This is true of newsstands, jewelry stores, and many other types of stores that find their display windows extremely valuable in selling to window shoppers. Usually these stores are better in downtown areas where pedestrian traffic is heavy.

Other types of retail businesses such as department stores have recently shown a tendency to move into shopping centers away from the downtown area. If the department store is large enough, it can attract business on its own.

Also in recent years, there has been a tremendous development of shopping centers which, in many cases, become a miniature downtown area within themselves. These shopping centers must be well located in relation to residential areas and accessible streets. It is also very helpful if the shopping center location is in a place where it does not have to compete with other and larger shopping centers in the vicinity. In some locations, there has been an overdevelopment of shopping centers with too many of them too close together. Where this condition exists, the shopping center that is the largest and has the most complete shopping facilities is usually the one that gets the most business. In some areas, there will be several competing shopping centers all doing a good business, but where there is no large shopping center. The fact that the several centers are prosperous and doing business indicates the need for a large shopping center, and in this case, it can be very profitable to locate a large tract of land which can be used for such purposes.

PROPERTY AND IMPROVEMENTS SUITABLE FOR TENANT

Every tenant has different requirements, but there are certain aspects that are important to all of them. In choosing properties to list or to buy, it is to your advantage to pick the ones which are most suitable for the greatest number of prospective tenants. You can evaluate very quickly the desirability of various types of property.

Residential Property

There are some types of residential property that rent more readily than others. From the viewpoint of the broker who is engaged in renting property to make money, apartments are usually the best. The reason for this is that he has so many more rental units, and his commission can run that much more. The important thing from the broker's standpoint is to get an exclusive listing on the apartment house, so that he can lease all the apartments in the building. In some areas, efficiency apartments rent better than any other type, and in other places, one or two bedrooms rent the best. Generally speaking, there is not too much demand for three-bedroom apartments, but there are exceptions.

The condition of the property is also of great importance. If the landlord is not keeping the property in good condition and not maintaining it as it should be, it will be more difficult to rent. It is also important to learn whether or not the utilities are furnished, and what is the condition of the heating equipment. Most of the new apartments built now are air-conditioned, and it is difficult to rent apartments that aren't. You should also notice whether the apartment has such attractive features as swimming pools or recreation rooms or anything else that would make it more attractive to the prospective tenant. A high proportion of tenants looking for apartment houses are young people, and a great many of them prefer the apartments to be furnished. It is generally accepted by apartment owners that those which are furnished rent more easily, although there is a greater turnover of tenants.

Offices

The rental of offices is a very profitable business activity. As in the case of apartment houses, if you are a broker, the best thing to do is to get an exclusive listing for an office building, so that you can handle all the leasing for it. The important things to look for are how the building is maintained and whether or not the offices are modern, well lighted, air-conditioned and heated. It is also of interest to you to know whether or not the offices are flexible in the sense that you can rent a one-, two- or three-room office. A good many office buildings are arranged so that space of almost any size can be furnished to a tenant.

There is a great demand all over the country for warehouse space and in many cities there is a shortage of it. Here, the important thing is the condition of the property, the load factor of the floor and the construction of it as to whether or not it is fireproof. The tenant is interested in a property which has a sufficient load factor to sustain the weights that he will put on the floor, and which is as fireproof as possible, so he can keep his fire insurance rates low. It is helpful if the building has a sprinkler system. It is also important from a security angle to see how the building is constructed. On many types of storage, theft is a considerable factor, and you can rent warehouse space that is well protected better than you can others.

All warehouses require loading platforms either for freight cars or trucks, and in many cases both. If the property is located on a railroad, there should be a spur line to it and loading platforms, so that freight cars can be loaded and unloaded directly on the platforms. If it is not on a freight line, there should be several loading and unloading docks for trucks.

Vacant Land

Often the grade of vacant land is a very important consideration. Generally speaking, land which is very rough and hilly and requires a large amount of fill is not very attractive unless the location is extremely good or the price very low. Try to get land as level as possible. It is also essential that utility lines come near it and sanitary sewers. The overriding factor in vacant land is how inexpensively it can be prepared for building.

Commercial Property

There are many considerations that enter into the value of commercial property. Is the building well constructed? Does it have modern heating and air conditioning equipment? Modern store windows?

It is also important to know how flexible the property can be and how much it will cost to remodel it to suit a tenant. All tenants' requirements are different, and usually some changes are required in order to make a commercial property suitable for any particular tenant.

Most commercial properties require certain partitions for office or storage space. They also require loading docks, usually in the rear. Here again, as in the case of warehouses, the construction of the building as to whether or not it is fireproof and as theft proof as possible is very important. The size of the room to be rented is also important. Generally speaking, the larger the room, the easier it is to rent, especially if it can be subdivided, in case that becomes necessary. It actually doesn't pay very much to try to lease small rooms because the rental is low and they are sometimes difficult to lease.

UNINTERRUPTED USE

One of the things you must be able to offer a prospective tenant is the uninterrupted utilization of the property leased. In most cases, it is reasonably obvious that you can deliver continuous use of the property covered by the lease; but if there is any suspicion that something might arise to interrupt the occupancy, it would be a good idea to find out about it before wasting your time and effort in trying to obtain tenants. There are a number of things that can interrupt a tenant's occupancy, and it is very difficult to rent property where there is such a possibility. It is a good idea to steer clear of such situations.

Possibility of Condemnation

In the event of condemnation of the property for any reason, the use of the property by the tenant is, of course, automatically interrupted. Most leases have a clause to cover this possibility, and release the landlord from liability to the tenant in the event of such an occurrence. In all leases, there should be something to protect the landlord in case this happens to absolve him from the possibility of a damage claim from the tenant.

One reason for condemnation procedure is if the property is in the path of a proposed street or highway. In this case it would be condemned by the state or federal government, whichever is involved, purchased from the owner and any improvements removed from it. The same thing can happen in the event of urban renewal. If the property is in the path of urban renewal, it would be a good idea to find out all particulars and see what the likelihood is that the property will be torn down to make room for new improvements.

Another reason for condemnation of property includes the existence of defects in construction such that would make it dangerous for the type of use to which it is employed. Frequently the various defects can be corrected by the owner and, if there is a provision in the lease to cover such a contingency, you can go ahead and make a reasonably long-term lease on the property. A long-term lease is always a desirable thing from the broker's standpoint, since it is the only means by which he can earn large lease commissions. It is also desirable to the owner because of continuity of income and availability of better financing.

Zoning Laws and Regulations

It is very important for everyone who is intending to lease property to be familiar with the zoning laws and regulations in his area. He certainly should have a zoning map showing the correct zoning of every piece of property in the city in which he is working. Sometimes these laws and regulations are quite stringent, and in some cases quite complex. Unless the use to which the tenant wishes to put the property complies with the zoning regulations of that particular property, he will find it impossible to enjoy uninterrupted use of it. For instance, it wouldn't do to rent space to a storage company for warehouse purposes in an area that is zoned only for residential or retail business purposes. In the event a lease is made, the tenant would find it impossible to use the property for the purpose for which he bargained for it and would, in all probability, be able to cancel the lease. Copies of all zoning laws and regulations can be obtained from the local zoning and planning commission, as well as a map showing what the zoning is on every piece of property in your area.

Adjustment Boards

Frequently if property is not suitable for a certain purpose due to zoning, a change can be effected by the adjustment board in your area. If the change desired is minor and does not involve a change in zoning policy, the board may have the power to make the change wished and will, in many cases, do so. The procedure in appearing before the board of adjustment and getting these changes made sometimes involves several weeks or months and much time on everybody's part. Unless the property that you are listing for lease is a large one and you think you can make a long-term sizable lease, it is probably not worth your time to bother with it if there is a question of zoning involved, even though you think changes can be obtained from the board of adjustment. There are too many properties available for lease, and there are too many investors who are interested in building for good tenants on leases, so that it isn't worthwhile for you to spend time on property that is of doubtful suitability.

PARKING

One of the most important considerations in any kind of property for lease is the availability of suitable parking. In some cases, parking is primarily needed for employees, and in others it is more important for the use of customers. With the tremendous use of automobiles for personal transportation, the matter of parking enters very prominently in any consideration of the suitability of property for lease.

Residential Property

The need for large parking areas is especially evident in the leasing of apartments. Frequently, especially in high-rise apartments, street parking is not sufficient to take care of the needs of the tenants. In most apartments, more parking spaces are needed than the number of apartments indicates. Some of the tenants will have more than one car and hence need extra parking space. Most of them will have guests from time to time that also need a place in which to leave cars.

The same is true, to a lesser extent, of single family homes. If the home you have for rent is jammed up against others and there is no place for parking, you are going to have a difficult time renting it. Of course there is the desirability of garages with single family homes, so that the tenant will have a place in which to leave his car protected from the weather.

Industrial Property

In the case of warehouses or industrial concerns, parking for the employees is of the primary consideration. Parking for trucks delivering or picking up merchandise does not require a great deal of space, since they do not remain long. However, it is a phenomenon of American industry today that nearly every employee comes to work in an automobile. For this reason, sufficient parking space for cars is required and should be near the plant to save time in getting to and from the cars. It is almost impossible, unless there are very few employees, for ordinary street parking to be of any benefit. In considering whether or not to lease property of this kind, a parking area is one of the most important things to consider.

Commercial Properties

Parking is probably of more importance in connection with commercial properties than with any other. It is true of office buildings, where there must be parking not only for the employees of the building, but also for people calling on the offices. For stores that sell merchandise at retail, parking is of even more importance.

It is generally considered that in shopping centers or in suburban stores, there should be a parking ratio of at least three to one. By this is meant that the parking area should be a minimum of three times as large as the floor area of the retail concerns. In many cities, this is the requirement of the zoning commission pertaining to shopping centers. It is also very important in downtown property that the location be convenient to parking lots or else that there must be much street parking.

In the case of suburban stores and shopping centers, the parking lot must be blacktopped, and there must be every reason to believe that it will be properly maintained. Some landlords maintain the parking lot and keep it well lighted and cleaned, and this makes the area much more attractive from the viewpoint of obtaining good tenants. If the landlord is careless and allows the blacktop to deteriorate and fails to keep it properly lighted and free from debris, it will be an uphill battle to make good leases in such an area.

Frequently leases for stores in shopping centers or suburban areas specify that the landlord is required to maintain the parking lot. In some leases, it is specified that each tenant shall keep up his proportioned part of the parking lot. In any event, there must be some assurance that the tenant will have uninterrupted use of sufficient parking for his business needs.

Another important point about parking areas is that there be unimpeded use of them. Frequently there will be nearby stores with drive-in service windows or parcel pick-up areas which cause traffic to back up and sometimes interfere with the parking spaces that should be allotted for other tenants. This is well worth considering and as it is necessary in order for you to obtain good tenants, you should be able to offer them uninterrupted continuous use of an adequate parking area.

OTHER THINGS THAT CAN INTERRUPT CONTINUOUS OCCUPANCY

There are various contingencies that can arise that would make continuous occupancy by the tenant for the purpose that he has in mind impossible. In most cases, it is obvious that none of these are likely to arise, but if there does seem a possibility of such, you should look into it carefully.

Residential Property

One of the worst things that can develop in leasing is the presence of nearby public nuisances. In some areas, residential areas are near disposal plants, meat-packing plants, chemical plants or other installations which cause unpleasant odors. It is difficult to rent property in such areas, due to the undesirability of the location. Other nuisances, from the viewpoint of people living in those areas, include excessive noise from highways, especially those that carry a large amount of fast truck traffic. The proximity to a rail line is also another source of annoyance, and it is usually difficult to rent property which is immediately adjoining an active railroad right-of-way.

Another consideration is the question of neighbors. If the neighbors are obviously undesirable, the property is not suitable for leasing. Of course, there are many areas where all of the considerations mentioned in this section apply, but these are slum areas and it certainly isn't worth while to try to rent property in such areas.

Commercial Property

The conditions that can make a commercial location unsuitable for leasing are often the same ones that apply to residential property. Other considerations would involve how well other commercial properties in the area are maintained. If the area is allowed to run down, it would be difficult for you to make an attractive lease. There is also the matter of visibility. If the property you have for lease is situated in such a way that the view of it is blocked by other businesses in the area, it becomes unsuitable for most prospective tenants.

In some shopping areas, especially in shopping centers under the same ownership, there is frequently a desire to keep competition in the area to a minimum. If you are looking for a location for a one-hour cleaner and there are already two or three in the area, you usually are wasting your time by trying to rent space to another one. In shopping centers, some stores will be granted an exclusive clause in their lease which makes it impossible for competing businesses to operate. Sometimes the owner is not aware of these clauses himself, and unless there is some research done to determine whether or not they exist, it might be possible that you will waste much time trying to make a lease that could not possibly be finalized.

POINTS TO KEEP IN MIND

Be sure that the property that you are going to work on is suitable for leasing and is in such condition that it is possible to obtain tenants.

- *Location.* Be sure that the location is attractive to prospective tenants.
- *Property and improvements suitable for tenants.* Be sure that the property is in good condition and has modern improvements on it so that you will not encounter unusual difficulties in leasing it.
- *Uninterrupted use.* Be certain that it is possible for the tenant to enjoy uninterrupted use of the property.
- *Parking.* Facilities for parking are very important and the more parking you have, the easier it will be to lease a property.

Chapter 2

Getting More for Your Advertising Dollar

If you are a broker, some of your advertising will be placed in order to obtain property for lease. When you start in the leasing business, you first need listings. Advertising for properties to lease can be in many forms, such as newspaper, magazine, direct mail, direct telephone or personal calls. However, whether you are a broker or not, most of your advertising will be to attract tenants for the properties you wish to lease. Advertising is the cheapest way of getting in touch with a number of prospects in the shortest possible time.

SIGNS

For anyone seeking prospective tenants, signs are a necessity. They attract the attention of people who are seeking locations to lease, and they give extensive exposure to the message which is conveyed.

Location

There are different spots in which signs are most advantageously displayed, according to the property advertised. For residential property, it is usually best to have the sign in the front yard of the house. For apartment house developments, the sign should be near the entrance to the development. For commercial properties, the location would depend on the type and size of the property involved.

For stores on the main street or in built-up areas, it is best to put the sign in the window of the store. If the store is a suburban one, perhaps it should be on a billboard in the parking lot. For shopping centers, it should be a sign in the parking lot that is easily seen from cars passing by.

Size of Signs

The size of the sign should, of course, be proportionate to the value of the property that is being advertised. In the case of a single family residence, it should be a small but attractive sign that can be read from traffic on the street. For the apartment house developments, the sign should be much larger and more attractive, since the value of the property to be leased is such that you can well afford a large sign.

On commercial properties, if it is a store building in an area where there is heavy pedestrian traffic, the sign does not have to be large but can be a small, inexpensive cardboard sign placed in the window of the store. If the property advertised is a warehouse or a large suburban store, then the sign would have to be larger and more impressive in proportion to the value of the property that you are trying to lease.

If you have a large tract of land that you are attempting to lease, either for development of a shopping center, for agricultural purposes or for motel development, the size of the sign should be quite large in order to be read by fast-moving traffic. The value of the property leased and the profit you will earn from it fully justify the investment of a considerable sum in the sign, and the fact that traffic on the highways is moving rapidly requires a large sign in order to be visible.

Wording of Signs

The major consideration in determining how to word a sign is visibility and size of sign so that the message on it can be quickly determined. One of the greatest mistakes people make in writing signs is putting too many words on it. If the sign is too filled, the average passer-by will not be able to read the entire message. If the sign is placed in a window of a store for pedestrian traffic, the sign can have more words on it, since the people walking by can stop in front of the window and read it. If the sign is on a highway location, the wording must be proportioned to the size of the sign, so the message can be read by highspeed traffic.

The important points to cover on the sign include the fact that the property is for lease and your name, address and phone number. The phone number should be very large, so it can be easily read. It is a good idea to have the signs made in contrasting colors, so these things stand out.

Recently, we had some valuable property in a neighboring town on which we were not getting any inquiries. The property was on a very busy highway and many people passed there everyday. It was on a highspeed road, so it was necessary to make the sign easy to read from cars traveling sixty miles per hour. The copy on the sign simply said, "Will Build to Suit Tenant," then the name, town and phone number.

Since putting this simple sign on the property, we have had quite a number of inquiries which I am sure will lead to development of the location.

NEWSPAPER ADVERTISING

You will probably reach more people with newspaper advertising than with any other medium. Of course, most people are not interested in your message, so newspaper advertising is largely a shotgun approach to the matter of finding prospects. However, it is necessary and is certainly a valuable tool to use.

Location of Ads Within Newspapers

The logical location for most "For Lease" ads is the classified section. There are usually several classifications concerning various types of property, such as: "Apartments for Rent," "Houses for Rent," "Business Locations for Rent"; etc. The classified section would probably take care of the great majority of your needs.

However, in the case of large industrial properties, shopping centers or large warehouses, it might be advisable to use a display ad. This ad should be on the financial page where it will attract the attention of most business people. The size of the ad should, of course, be in proportion to the size and importance of the property that is advertised.

It is frequently worthwhile for a broker to put a general institutional type of ad, advertising his own services on the financial page.

This can be a small ad, mentioning only the fact that he is a lease specialist. By being on the financial page, an ad like this will call attention to people who own property that you are specializing in leases, and might be a good source of listings for you.

One good magazine to use for this purpose is the *Chain Store Age*, Shopping Center Edition. A friend of mine in the real estate business put such an ad in this magazine and tells me he received twenty-five inquiries from firms who were interested in locating in his area.

Such an ad might appear as follows:

> Regional Shopping Center Now Leasing. Large Southeastern Market. Fine Location and Center of 150,000 Prosperous People. Your Name, Address and Phone Number.

How to Word Advertisements

Classified ads do not require many words. A small ad frequently does as well as a large one and costs much less. It is important, however, that the ad be put under the proper classification, and it is frequently desirable to have the first line in bold type. This first line should give a definite indication of what is for lease. It should be specific enough so that someone reading the ad can immediately detect if it is anything of interest to him. In the case of a house, the first line could be, **"Attractive 8-Room Home"** or whatever size the home is. The same thing would be true of apartments. A description should be put in the first line so that the average reader knows whether there is any need for him to read the rest of the ad. For office space, it could read, **"3-Room Office," "4-Room Office"** or whatever may be applicable.

If you have many commercial properties, there is some advantage in not giving the size of the storeroom in your ads. If the storeroom that you wish to advertise is 3,000 square feet and you mention that fact in the ad, then you will not get inquiries from anyone who wants a smaller or larger area. By not putting the size in the ads, you can make the ads serve a double purpose by not only getting prospects for the specific property you are advertising, but also for others which you may have available.

Parking is such an important feature in commercial leases that it is usually a good idea, if there is plenty of parking, to mention in your first bold type line something about ample parking or words to that effect. Generally speaking, in all commercial ads, the ad should be clear, brief and as much to the point as possible.

MAGAZINE ADVERTISING

Newspaper advertising and signs are shotgun methods of advertising, in that they attract the attention of many people, only a few of whom are actual prospects. However, magazine advertising can be slanted directly to the people who are most likely to be interested. Not as many people will see it, but the group that does see it will be composed of people who are interested in your message.

Magazines to Use

For advertising business space to lease, trade magazines are the logical medium to use. There are trade magazines for all industries. For instance, there is one that is exclusively devoted to shopping centers and chain stores, *Chain Store Age,* combined with *Shopping Center Age.* To advertise an entire shopping center, this would be a logical medium. If you wish drug tenants, the trade magazine for the drug industry is *Drug Topics.* Practically every industry has a trade magazine, and by asking friends who are in that particular business, you can easily discover which are the best ones. By advertising in these magazines, you reach the people who are interested in the exact thing that you have to offer.

As far as residential property is concerned, it would be very unusual if you could use a magazine, but in some types of very high-priced and unique properties, this is suitable. Sometimes it is desirable to put ads in some magazines regarding apartment property. If a large industry is moving to your city and bringing a number of employees with it, you should attempt to place an ad in the house magazine published by that company. If it is a large company, it undoubtedly publishes such a magazine and will be glad to put an ad in it of your apartment development because the company is, of course, interested in finding good accommodations for the workers it is bringing into your city. If you are advertising farms for rent, there are a number of agricultural magazines that might be of interest to you. In advertising land for rent for the purpose of motels or restaurants, there are also several magazines in this field. The *Tourist Court Journal* is probably the most widely circulated magazine going to the motel industry.

A few years ago, we put a very simple ad in this magazine which read as follows:

> Motel. New and modern. Near Interstate Interchange. Gross room rentals over $100,000 per year. Cash required for purchase only $75,000.

As a result of this one ad, we had several inquiries and sold the motel for a total price of $350,000, with a resulting commission of $17,500.

Cost and Wording

At first, you may think that magazine advertising would be unusually expensive. However, such is not the case, because frequently you can advertise in magazines at a lower cost than you can in some newspapers. This is especially true of trade papers which do not have a very wide circulation, but that do reach the customers that you wish to reach.

Since your ads in trade papers are designed for business people in a particular line of business, the ads can be brief and factual, with enough indication to arouse the prospect's interest. It is not necessary to waste space with glowing adjectives or generalized statements, as your average reader will pay very little attention to these things. To the reader of a trade magazine, time usually is at a premium and he is more apt to read a short ad which is to the point and which gives the salient facts. He will be more favorably inclined to an advertiser who words his ads so as to give him as much information at a glance as is possible.

DIRECT MAIL ADVERTISING

Of all types of advertising, other than a personal call, direct mail advertising is the most expensive per contact. It can be the most concentrated, however, since the mailing can be to people who are likely to be interested, thus reducing waste. While fewer people are contacted by direct mail than by newspaper or by billboard advertising, fewer of the contacts are wasted due to complete lack of interest. Not all types of property can be easily advertised by direct mail, although some kinds are well suited to this type of advertising.

Uses of Direct Mail

It is not often that you can advertise residential property of any kind by the direct mail method. However, occasionally when a new industry is moving to your area, it would pay to mail letters to the employees who are transferred from some other area. These people transferred to your area are not familiar with it and are very susceptible to advice by local brokers who are in a position to know what neighborhoods are best and what types of rental property are available. Most of these people are dependent on the help of someone in finding them a place to live. Such a mailing can be very profitable and result in the rental of many homes.

In attempting to lease office space, direct mailings are frequently of value. If your office space location is such that it would be of value to insurance companies, you could send a letter to various companies that might be interested in using space in your area. If your office space is especially adapted to any other kind of business, you can make a mailing to members of that particular business. Sometimes office space near hospitals is especially desirable for doctors, and a mailing to a list of doctors might be very worthwhile.

Commercial buildings probably lend themselves to direct mail method of advertising more than any other type of property. If the property that you wish to lease is a storage warehouse, you can write to the various businesses in your area that are expanding and might need extra storage space. If the property you have for lease is a store building on the main street, you could write to various chain stores that you think might be interested in moving. If your property is in a good location on a main highway that would be suitable for a service station, you can write to all of the oil companies that are not already represented in that immediate area. The big advantage of direct mail advertising is that it can be tailored to fit any particular situation.

Direct mail advertising is especially valuable in the event you are leasing and trying to find tenants for a shopping center. You can mail letters to the types of businesses that you want in your shopping center and to the ones that you think are interested in expanding in your area. Since all of the stores in a planned shopping center are new ones, you should be interested in companies which are expanding and interested in putting branches in your area. By this method you can save time by discussing the shopping center only with people who would logically be interested in locating there. On the other side of the coin, you can also save time by not contacting the businesses that you do not need or do not want in the shopping center.

A sample letter of this type would be Exhibit 2-1.

Mr. A. O. Smith
Director of Real Estate
C & D Company
New York, New York

Dear Mr. Smith:

You are to be congratulated on the fine new stores that you are opening in this general area.

Certainly you should have one of these stores in our Eastern Park Shopping Center. Our center will be the only one in an area with over 200,000 people and will have easy access from all directions.

We have completed trade surveys of the area and architect's drawing showing 130,000 square feet of retail area with room for parking 2,000 cars. In our center, we will have one large and one small department store and the usual assortment of other tenants.

Our time schedule calls for starting construction of this center in about six months and opening it about the first of March, in the year after next. A map showing the location of our center is enclosed.

We have complete trade surveys of the area and architect's drawings of our floor plan for the center. If you are interested and would like to receive this information, let us know.

Very truly yours,

Preliminary Shopping Center Letter

Exhibit 2-1

How to Get Mailing Lists of Names

Companies who are moving a large number of employees to your area from some other area are quite anxious to find adequate housing for these people. If you will contact the personnel director of the corporation involved and sell him on the value of your services in getting his people located in their new area, he will give you a list of the employees who are being transferred.

One of the greatest sources of mailing lists of all kinds is the telephone directory. You can go through this directory and get lists of people who might be interested in office space or in warehouse space. It is also possible to get a list of any type of business, since they are already classified in the yellow pages.

There are all kinds of mailing lists that can be purchased from firms who specialize in selling such lists. None of these lists are entirely up to date, and there will be some names with incorrect addresses and thus a certain amount of waste. However, usually the lists are about 75 or 80 percent correct. From your telephone directory, you will find about 95 percent accuracy.

For a list of chain stores that you might want to contact, you should obtain the current directory of leading chain stores in the United States. This book can be obtained from the National Association of Real Estate Boards or from the Chain Store Business Guide Company, published at 2 Park Avenue, New York, New York. This book has several classifications including supermarkets, drug stores, shoe stores, etc. Under these various classifications, it lists the names and addresses of the leading chains and the number of stores each chain has in the area of the United States that is covered. By going through these lists and picking out the ones that are in areas near you, you can come up with a surprisingly accurate list of chains who might be interested in moving into your territory. On one mailing of this kind, we were surprised to find that out of twenty-eight letters mailed, we received fifteen replies. This is an unusually high percentage of replies, but the letters were directed to people who were logically interested in what we were writing about.

TELEPHONE CONTACTS

The big advantage of telephone calls is the fact that it is a personalized method of advertising. If you can arouse a person's interest over the phone to the extent that he asks you questions, it gives you a chance to overcome any objections the prospective tenant may have. It also gives you a chance to find out what his requirements are and to determine whether or not you can furnish what he needs.

Follow-ups

Probably the best use that can be made of telephone calls is to follow up inquiries received from advertisements or to follow up direct mailings. One of the best procedures we know of to obtain prospects is to first send them a letter or a brochure by mail. Allow for the time it takes for them to receive this, and then call by phone. This gives them a chance to actually see your name in print and get a good idea of what you have to offer. Then when you make the telephone call, you are not calling as a complete stranger because they will, no doubt, recognize your name and have some advance notice of what you want to talk with them about. Some of the most successful sales campaigns in finding prospective tenants that we have ever made have been done in this manner.

Of course the telephone is an ideal follow-up for inquiries that you have received from the result of direct mail campaigns or from advertisements in the newspapers or on signs or any other medium. It is very difficult to get a prospect's complete attention when you call him on a cold canvass deal. In this case, unless you know the person personally, both your name and purpose will be unfamiliar to him. He may be busy at the time that you call, in which case his primary interest would be in getting back to whatever he was doing before you called him. For this reason, I recommend telephone calls primarily as follow-ups.

Small Leases

What I mean by small leases is a lease for a small amount of money, for a short length of time and in which the profit is very small. In property of this kind, it does not pay you to spend a great deal of effort and time or money in trying to find tenants. For that reason, it sometimes is not worthwhile to advertise in any fashion to get prospects other than by signs. However you can spend a few minutes over the telephone calling people that would be logical prospects and some times complete a deal over the phone with very little expenditure of time or money on your part. In fact sometimes telephone calls, if you can narrow your list of prospects down to a few, are the least expensive and quickest way of leasing small properties.

PERSONAL CALLS

Probably the most effective of all types of advertising is a personal call on a logical prospective tenant.

Follow-ups

As in the case of telephone calls, a personal call is put to best advantage when it is a follow-up of a mail order campaign or to inquiries that have been received from some other type of advertising. When you send your card to a prospective tenant and he recognizes your name from having recently seen it on a letterhead or in an advertisement, you have gained a tremendous advantage. Certainly the personal call is the most effective follow-up, as it carries much more emphasis and much more weight than any other method.

Personal Calls Proportioned to Value

Personal calls are quite time consuming and sometimes involve much automobile or travel expense. For that reason, the amount of time and money you spend on personal calls should be proportioned to the size of profit that you stand to gain. On large deals such as a department store on a fifteen- or twenty-year lease, it would pay you to make a trip to anywhere in the nation, if you have a logical prospect. Whether or not it is worthwhile to make a personal call on a prospect is a matter of judgment as each case arises.

POINTS TO KEEP IN MIND

- *Signs.* The important thing about signs is the proper location and a concise message. Use as few words as possible.
- *Newspaper.* Be sure to place your ad in the paper which people who will be interested in your type of property are most likely to read. Make the first sentence in your ad stand out and attract the readers' interest.
- *Direct Mail.* The important thing about direct mail advertising is your mailing list. Fit the letter on one page, if possible, and your first paragraph especially should arouse the reader's interest.
- *Telephone Calls.* The best use of telephone calls is a follow-up to other advertising to answer inquiries. Frequently they are used as a means of setting up appointments to contact the prospect personally.
- *Personal Calls.* By all means make an appointment in advance if you are calling on busy people. Frequently personal calls are used as a follow-up to answer inquiries received from other forms of advertising.

Chapter 3

How to Overcome Objections and Get Leases Signed

There are several very strong reasons why all leases should be in writing and in the proper form. No agreement pertaining to real estate is valid and enforceable in law unless it is in writing. It is also true that all leases cover a period of time which sometimes can be quite lengthy. It is difficult for either party to remember the particulars of a lease for the time covered by the instrument. If it is a very long lease and especially a commercial one, the signatures of both parties should be notarized.

HAVE LEASES READY

If you are negotiating a lease between a property owner and a realistic tenant, it is always advisable to have a lease ready for both to sign as soon as possible after an agreement has been reached.

Standard Forms

For residential property, especially apartments, there are standardized forms that can be purchased at almost any stationery store. If these are suitable to the landlord for whom you are soliciting tenants, you should have a stock of these forms on hand at all times. These forms cover the important things which should be carefully specified in all leases. There are certain points that are essential to any lease agreement regardless of the kind of property or the terms of the lease. These are:

Description of premises leased
Length of lease
Renewal options, if any
Amount of rental
When rental payments are due
Tenant guaranteed peaceful possession
Premises to be used only for lawful purposes
Tenant shall not be a public nuisance
Conditions under which lease can be cancelled
Signature of both parties

There are a number of other points that might be and generally are in standard leases, but the above are the really important ones. Any standard leases that you can buy at the stationery store allow plenty of space to fill in the landlord's name and the tenant's name. They also allow plenty of space to fill in a description of the property to be leased, the amount of rental and the terms of payment.

The important thing about having these stock lease forms on hand is that you will have one available for the tenant to sign immediately, because in effecting leases, as in other matters, the time to get a prospect to sign is when he is in the mood to do so.

Unusual Lease Provisions

Sometimes there are local conditions that require special treatment in the lease, and a stock form will not be suitable. Also frequently there are unusual provisions that the landlord or the tenant wants to put in, or sometimes both of them wish to make different provisions. Sometimes one or the other of them will object to the wording of a standard form lease, but will agree on different wording. It is usually possible to fill in these changes on a standard lease form without the necessity of typing an entirely new lease. Where these changes are typed on a standard lease form, it should be initialed by both parties.

Some of the unusual and variable things in residential leases are as follows:

Restrictions against pets.

Sometimes, especially in certain apartment developments, there is a restriction against children of a certain age.

Approved provisions for a grace period before a tenant can be evicted for nonpayment of rent.

Responsibility for maintenance of heating and air conditioning equipment when it is different from the clause in a standard lease.

Sometimes the frequency with which the landlord is to redecorate is set out in the lease.

Any contingent changes in the amount of the rental due to a change in the cost of living index or a change in property taxes.

Clauses pertaining to the maintenance and repair of furniture where the home or apartment is rented completely furnished. Many leases will have a clause in them requiring the tenant to maintain all furniture in as good a condition as when leased, ordinary wear and tear excepted.

There are a number of other clauses that might have to be changed or additional clauses inserted, but the important thing is to be prepared to make these changes promptly. If there is any undue delay in getting the lease ready, the tenant might use this delay to find other property, and the time you used in getting him interested in the lease proposition is entirely wasted.

OBJECTIONS TO SIGNING AND HOW TO OVERCOME

Since the lease actually is not a reality until it is signed by both parties, it is important that you obtain their signatures. Usually there is no problem connected with the lessor, since you know what he wants before you start seeking tenants and because he is usually anxious to get his property leased so that rental income can start as soon as possible. The signature that is important to get as promptly as possible before he has a chance to change his mind is the prospective tenant. As soon as an agreement is reached, a lease should be presented to the tenant and a fountain pen given him so that he can sign immediately.

There are various objections that the prospect might think of to delay signing the lease.

Lease Commits Me Too Long

This objection is quite often mentioned in anything other than a month-to-month lease. Most landlords desire a term lease, especially if their property is desirable, and these term leases sometimes run anywhere from six months to eighteen months. This objection is mentioned most frequently on leases of one year or longer. You can answer such an objection in the following suggested manner:

"Don't forget that this lease also guarantees you continuous uninterrupted possession of this home for the period of time stated. Properties like this are not often available for rent, as you have probably already discovered. You might look a long time and not find another one with the desirable features that this has. Besides you know how much time and trouble is involved in finding a place that you like. And it is expensive to move too.

"If you intend to stay in this locality as long as the period of time mentioned in this lease, there is a definite advantage in being settled and assured of a nice place to live for this length of time. You can get to know people in this nice neighborhood and enjoy your stay here without the possibility of being disrupted and of finding it necessary to look for another place."

Don't Understand Contract

Usually an objection like this is merely a cover-up for some other kind of objection that your prospective tenant has in mind. Sometimes, however, he actually means what he says when he says that he does not understand the contract, and the best way for you to answer this objection is something like this:

"A lawyer sometimes can put things in language that is difficult to understand. However, the language in this lease is not so difficult but what with a minimum of study you can understand it clearly. Most of this lease is a stock form that is used in making thousands of leases by people all over the country, and there are no unusual provisions in it.

"It is necessary to have a certain minimum number of provisions in any rental contract as I am sure you realize. This contract has as few of these provisions as any of them, and it is drawn not only for the protection of the landlord, but also for your protection as a tenant as well. Would you like to go over this contract paragraph by paragraph, even the part that is printed and is common to all lease contracts? If so, we can do that in a very few minutes.

"Actually this standard lease contract is something that has evolved over many years of use and has been proven to be fair to both parties. No lease contract or any other type of contract could be in continuous use unless it were a fair and equitable one.

"Why don't you just glance at this paragraph by paragraph, and for anything that you do not understand, let me know and I can explain it. I think if you will read it with care you will have no trouble understanding it unless there may be some legal phrases that are not very clear to anyone other than an attorney."

I Don't Want to Put It in Writing

Sometimes this objection is a sign of bad faith on the part of your prospective tenant. If you size him up as such, the best thing to do is to forget it and find yourself another prospect. However, sometimes this objection is voiced by people whose intentions are good but who are frightened by any legal-looking document. It may be that they do not have a very good education, or they may in the past have had a bad experience in signing a contract. Usually this argument is fairly easy to overcome, and you can answer this objection in a number of different manners. One of them is suggested below:

"Since by law no contract relating to real estate is valid unless in writing, a lease arrangement made on this property wouldn't mean anything unless it were reduced to writing. For this reason, it is of advantage to both parties to have the terms of the lease put in permanent written form. There are certain things that you want as a result of this lease and, in actuality, you would not be assured of them unless the contract were in writing.

"You want to be assured of continuous peaceful occupation of these premises, and you want to be assured that the rent will not be raised during the term of the lease. Neither of these things would be assured on a purely verbal contract because it would not be legally binding on anyone. You also want to be assured that the landlord will keep the premises in a state of repair such as to keep it usable for residential purposes. This can only be guaranteed to you with a written contract.

"There are quite literally millions of lease contracts made every year, and virtually all of these are written contracts. If you find a property that you can rent on a verbal contract, you will find a property that is not too desirable in the first place. You would also realize that, since a contract pertaining to real estate is not valid unless in writing, you will only have a month-to-month lease. It means that the landlord can terminate your lease at any time and require you to move out whether you want to or not.

"Another reason why all of these contracts should be in writing is the fact that people are human and have faulty memories. I am sure you would feel very bad if you found out after moving in that the owner had remembered the rent to be higher than you had thought. The particular landlord who owns this property also owns a great many other properties, and it is not easy to carry all these matters in his head.

"I do not know what disadvantages there might be in putting it in writing; frankly I cannot think of any. If the two parties make an agreement in good faith, it certainly is not disadvantageous to either one of them to put the contract in writing. It is only by putting it in writing that they can be assured of remembering the terms of the contract correctly and the only way they can be assured of each having a record of what the terms of the contract were."

CLOSING METHODS

Since no lease is completed until signed by everyone, this is the final step that completes the lease contract. It is always highly disappointing and time wasting to follow through on a lease deal up to the point where the prospect is to sign and then find that he does not do so. Even though he says he is going to sign, but prefers to do so later, you actually do not accomplish anything until he does actually put his signature in writing on this contract. There are a number of methods of being sure that you get the prospect to sign at the time you want him to, and the exact one you use will depend on circumstances at the moment. It must always be remembered that if the lease is made to a man and wife, both of them must sign it.

Convenience

One of the most important points in getting leases signed is to have everything ready to make the signing itself convenient. The first requirement, of course, is to have the lease ready with any changes already made. The lease should be completely filled in with the name of the tenant, the term of the lease and the amount of the rent, so that there will be no delay in getting the lease ready when your prospects are in the mood to sign.

Occasionally contracts have been lost because of the lack of a convenient place on which to sign. Be sure that there is a desk or some other flat place convenient where it will be easy to lay the lease flat and write a signature. This should be convenient to both parties in the event that a man and wife are each signing the lease.

It is obvious that a good pen with plenty of ink be available. Occasionally a landlord will prefer that his leases be signed with a pen other than a ball point. In this case you should, by all means, have such a pen handy and give it to your prospect so that he will be sure to use the correct pen. However, remember to have a pen ready so that there will be no delay in hunting for one or finding ink in order for the lease to be signed.

Confidence

One of the simplest and most effective means of getting any contract signed is to take for granted that it is going to be signed. There should never be any doubt whatever in your mind that everything is not going ahead just fine, and if there are any doubts in your mind that the contract might not be signed, be sure that these doubts do not show.

In talking to a prospective tenant about the contract, never use such an expression as, "If you sign the contract . . . .," always say, "When this contract is completed . . . ." When everything is all settled and the prospect is ready to sign, put the lease before him and hand him a pen. Never say, "Will you sign here?" Merely put the pen in his hand, point out the place to sign and say, "Sign here." This method makes it very easy for the prospect to sign, and it is quite difficult for him to refuse.

The Choice Method

Another method of completely finishing the deal by getting the prospect's signature is the "choice" method. When everything is ready for the prospect to sign, be sure that he has two choices, either one of which results in his signing the contract. Never give him a choice as to whether to sign or not to sign, but simply choices in the methods of signing. This is usually very effective in getting quick action on signatures.

When the psychological moment comes and everything is all ready for signature, never say, "Are you now going to sign the contract?" This might imply some doubt in your mind as to whether or not he is going to sign and this, of course, you do not want to do. However, you can say something like, "Do you want to use your pen or mine?" Then whichever way he answers he signs the contract. In the event that two people sign the contract, another choice that can be given is which one is to sign first. You can simply ask, "Which one of you wishes to sign first?" Then when one indicates he or she is ready to sign, point to the line on which he is to sign and hand him a pen. There are other methods by which you can give the prospect a choice which may be appropriate at the time. It is important, however, to be sure that when you do give him a choice, both options are in your favor and result in a signature.

POINTS TO KEEP IN MIND

- Be certain to have a lease ready.
- Make the signing as convenient as possible by being properly prepared.
- Always assume that the lease is going to be signed.
- When necessary, use the choice method.

Chapter 4

Leasing Homes and Estates: How to Maximize Your Profits

Like most other divisions of the real estate business, the leasing of homes and estates is a separate division and has problems and techniques peculiar to that phase of the business. It is estimated that in any one calendar year, nearly 20 percent of all the people in the United States move from one location to another. This is the market that you are seeking in order to find tenants.

WHO ARE YOUR PROSPECTS?

For Homes

People looking for single family dwellings (as distinct from duplexes and apartments) are usually family people. Occasionally you will find a couple without children, but this is rare. Most of these people will be comparatively young, with children ranging in age from a few months up to the teens. The size of the families will run from those that have one child to those that have four or five.

These people are generally interested in the same things. A good neighborhood in which to raise their children and convenience to schools or school buses are two essential assets. The size of the property offered will, of course, be proportionate to the size of the family. In addition to looking for good neighborhoods and convenience to schools, these couples are concerned with how modern the home is and with the conveniences that it offers. Some of them are looking for relatively short leases and others for longer leases. The best customers for you are, of course, those looking for long-term leases because they are usually better tenants, and the leases are basically more satisfactory.

Many of the families will be looking for furnished homes. Should this be the case, you should be very careful to get references. Generally tenants who have their own furniture are much more to be desired than tenants that are looking for furnished homes.

Other prospects that you will encounter are people who plan to stay in a community on a seasonal basis. In some communities, especially in university towns, a number of the university professors and other employees like to be away in the summertime between school years. This means that their homes will sit vacant unless rented. It is generally a good idea to rent these homes, in order to effect a possible savings in insurance costs and to ensure that someone will be occupying the residence to take care of it. Of course, on the other hand, there may be people who live further south or somewhere else and would like to live in your area during the summertime. These people must be screened carefully, since they will be occupying someone's home. Frequently the rent in these cases can be very reasonable due to the owner's desire to have someone in the house while he is away. These types of tenants are different from the other types in that they will usually be couples without children.

Estates

By estates I mean large properties usually consisting of very large homes and, in some cases, several hundred acres of land. This sort of property is very expensive and, of course, the rentals would be very high. Estates are for rent at various times for various reasons. Frequently when the original owner dies, none of the heirs particularly want to live on the property, and they find it difficult to divide the property among themselves. For this reason, it is frequently leased out as the most satisfactory way of maintaining the property and receiving an income from it. People who are interested in leasing estates are people with large incomes who do not expect to be in that particular locality for any great period of time. While there, they would like to have the best of everything, but do not like to make the permanent investment in buying an estate as they realize their residency will be a matter of only a few years.

Other rental prospects for estates are people who intend to make a business of some kind out of the property. Some of these are adaptable for resorts of various kinds. The tenant can, by a few changes, make the property suitable for a deluxe hotel, renting rooms and serving meals. It can have in conjunction with it, bridle paths, tennis courts or perhaps even a golf course. Other commercial uses for it might include nursing homes or sanitariums. In these cases, the prospective tenant should and must have a long-term lease. Usually such leases are negotiated for a short period of years for the primary term with a number of options, so that the tenant is assured of uninterrupted use of the property for fifteen to twenty years. The primary term is designed so that it will give the tenant the opportunity to determine whether or not the idea is going to be worthwhile. Usually the first year or two of this sort of thing is not profitable, and if it looks as though the project will continue to be unprofitable, the tenant can vacate when the primary terms expire. On the other hand, should his effort and expense have turned it into a profitable enterprise, he is assured of continuous occupancy by the options in his lease.

Farms

There is a difference between a farm and an estate, because an estate is primarily for luxurious living, while a farm is a business enterprise. You will find quite a number of farms that can be rented either because the owner is incapacitated and cannot operate it himself or heirs to an estate may find that renting the farm out is the only thing they can do. People who are interested in renting farms are people who make a business of farming, but don't have the capital to purchase sufficient land. In recent years there has been a tendency for farms to grow, and with the advent of modern farm machinery, the small farmer is having a hard time competing with the larger ones. For that reason, the average professional farmer wants a large acreage which could entail a great deal of capital investment. The only way he can enter this type of business without the capital necessary to buy the large farm is to rent one.

Farming is different in different areas. In some areas of the country, farming consists, to a large extent, of raising vegetables; in others, farming will primarily consist of raising cattle or maybe horses. In others a more general type of farming is the case, where the tenant would raise various kinds of crops, as well as livestock such as cattle and sheep. It will not take you long to become familiar with the type of farming that prevails in your locality.

Since the purpose of renting a farm is to make a profit from it, the principal consideration in the viewpoint of the tenant is how profitable the farm can be to him. This often depends on the fertility of the soil, how well it is watered and whether it is flat or hilly.

Since the tenant farmer usually lives on the farm that he rents, whether or not there are conveniences available such as he finds in the city may be quite important.

Recently we were asked to find a tenant for a large farm for two or three years because the owners wished to hold it for a length of time before offering it for sale. By contacting the farm agent, we got the names of two or three active farmers who needed more land. One of these leased the land, and our commission on this lease amounted to several thousand dollars. In addition to that, when the time came to sell the land, we were able to get an exclusive listing on it.

HOW TO REACH THESE PROSPECTS

Newspaper Advertising

There are two types of advertising, institutional advertising and the advertising of specific properties. If you are a broker and plan to specialize in leasing homes and estates, it would be a good idea to have an institutional ad appear often. This ad should be under *Homes for Rent* in the classified section. It can be very brief and simply state something like this:

> Specialist in renting livable homes, your name, address and phone number.

The other type of advertising which directs the reader's attention to specific properties generally should also be in the classified section. In the case of very large properties such as an estate or a large farm, it might pay you to place a display ad. Generally speaking, classified ads on rental properties should be brief and to the point, and your name and phone number should be emphasized, perhaps in bold type. The important thing you are trying to associate in the reader's mind is rental property and your name and your phone number.

An ad could read something like this:

For Rent. Two-, three- or four-bedroom homes. Desirable location. Name, address, phone number.

Institutions

Frequently you can obtain a good list of prospective tenants from various institutional sources. One of these would be the Chamber of Commerce in your city. Many people who plan to move to a community will write to the Chamber of Commerce for information about where they can get a home, a farm, an estate or whatever it is they wish to lease. Usually the local Chamber of Commerce does not have any facilities for servicing these requests themselves and are very glad to turn them over to local persons. Naturally an owner or broker who is a member of the Chamber of Commerce will be favored in receiving these inquiries.

These inquiries are good ones since there is no doubt about the tenant moving to your community and wanting to rent some property there. Usually when these people write in, they will specify what size family they have, how large a property they need and often approximately how much they can afford to pay as rent. With this advance information about your prospect, you can save valuable time. By going through your files, you can quickly determine what properties might be of interest and can write these people that you do have properties suitable for them that you would like to show to them. In this type of letter we have found it generally best to mention as few details of the property as possible. All you are trying to accomplish in answering this inquiry is to get the prospective tenant to come to see you when he moves to your community. Putting unnecessary details in the letter wastes time needlessly, since the prospect is going to look at the property before he rents it anyway. There is also the possibility that you might mention some detail which is unimportant, but which might be something that the prospect doesn't like, and for that reason he may not come to see you at all.

Such a letter might read like Exhibit 4-1.

Dear Prospect:

We are glad to hear that you plan to move to our city of Donesville. You will find a nice community with many friendly people, and we would like to welcome you here.

In our business we specialize in leasing homes and apartments. Whatever the size or type of home or apartment you may need, I am sure we can fill the bill.

When you arrive in our city, we would appreciate your giving us a phone call, and we will immediately make arrangements to show you and your wife the various attractive locations that we have to offer.

Looking forward to hearing from you soon.

Sincerely yours,

Good-Will Letter to Expected New Residents

Exhibit 4-1

Any large industrial concern that employs a large number of people and sometimes transfers them into your locality from other localities can be an excellent source of prospects. You should get to know the personnel manager of the largest firms, and he will frequently tell you when they are moving people from one area to another. These firms are anxious for their employees to have nice places to live and if he finds out that you have something worthwhile to offer, he will automatically call you when he knows that they are transferring a number of people into your locality.

If you live in a college town, you will be able to get prospects from the school's business office. Nearly all of the colleges and universities are growing so fast that they have a housing problem. When new professors are moving in either permanently or temporarily, it is difficult to find places to live. The business office would be glad to have some reputable person help them out in this matter.

It quite frequently happens that parents of young people in school will rent a home in the school town for the period of enrollment. These are very good prospects and, here again, the cooperation of the Chamber of Commerce and of the local school is important, since it is through these agencies that you will get in touch with most of these people. An institutional type of advertisement in the newspaper is helpful, and it is generally advisable to place this type of advertising shortly before the opening of the school year.

Another good source of prospects for rental homes, if you are a broker, is to be found in cooperation with other brokers in your community. If you become known as a lease specialist, many of these brokers will bring prospects to you. This would be done on a "split-the-commission" basis. The general arrangement is this: if the broker bringing the prospect to you does half of the work, he will get half of the commission. If he simply refers the prospect to you and you do all the work, you should not give the cooperating broker more than 25 percent of the resulting commission.

Estates

The reasons why people look for estates differ from place to place. Sometimes the location of an estate near a large city is of interest to business people as a place to live from which they can commute to the city. If the estate listed with you is in this catagory, your best bet is an advertisement in a financial paper such as the *Wall Street Journal*, or in any other publications going to people of means. Frequently the owners of an estate who want to lease can give you leads to people who might be interested.

An estate might be desirable because of the fact that it has facilities for keeping horses and bridal paths or training tracks or other facilities where the horses can be ridden. This is true, to some extent, of almost every state in the union, but especially so in certain areas. Here again, the owners of the estate can frequently give you excellent leads as to whom you should contact. Other possible sources of leads would be magazines that go to horse lovers, and there are a number of these. There are different types of magazines concerned with different types of horses. There are several publications for saddle horses, and anyone who is interested in this sort of thing can tell you which are the best magazines. The same thing applies to trotting horses, race horses or any other kind.

If the estate is situated near a large center of population and is easily accessible by good roads, it can frequently be adapted to commercial use. The thing to do is to decide which commercial use you think is best. Frequently these are used as very high-priced resorts. If you think that would be the best use for it, your best bet would probably be an ad in a hotel management magazine which goes to owners and operators of this type of property. The property might be adaptable more easily to a rest home, something that is becoming more in demand in many parts of the country. A good source of prospects here would be a telephone directory, and you could send a direct mail piece to all of the rest home operators in your area. Due to a somewhat similar type of operation, an ad in a hotel management type of magazine would be of value here also.

Somewhat different from a rest home is a nursing home or convalescent hospital. An advertisement in a medical magazine that goes to doctors would be indicated here. It also might be of value to send a letter to a mailing list composed of doctors in your community. It would probably be a good idea to follow up this direct mail campaign by telephone calls to certain types of doctors. The ones in more expensive office locations are probably in better financial shape to do business. It also might be desirable to follow up all of those that are giving psychiatric treatment, as there is considerable demand for sanitariums for various types of mental or emotional trouble.

Farms

There are a great many different types of farms. In many areas of the country, the primary farming business is raising livestock and in others, various kinds of crops. Sometimes one crop is predominant, and the farming in that area is a highly specialized business. For general farming, where both crops and livestock are raised, there are a great number of sources for obtaining prospects. If there is a college or university in your city, the agricultural department head can frequently give you leads as to people who might be interested in leasing large farm properties. Another source of prospects would be banks. There are usually one or two banks that specialize in farm loans in a locality. The officers of these banks are familiar with what is going on in the rural areas and are usually familiar with the people who like large farm operations. Another excellent source of prospects would be your local office of the Agriculture Department of the federal government. These people are familiar with all the farm land in your community and usually are acquainted with most of the large operators. You can get some very valuable leads from the Farm Agent of the federal Department of Agriculture.

The farm may be specialized into certain crops. This is usually true in the Midwest, where some farms will raise mainly wheat, corn or both, plus some other crop such as soy beans. Here again, a good source of prospects would be the same as for general farming; that is, schools, banks, the federal Department of Agriculture, and agricultural magazines that go to people interested in this type of farming. A few inquiries can give you information as to which magazines are circulated most widely in your locality, and an ad in these will frequently be of value.

On farms that specialize in livestock, there are some that specialize in raising cattle, some in sheep, some in hogs and some in horses of various kinds. Here again, magazine advertising is valuable, and you can find out which circulate best in your area. There are magazines that are of interest to cattle ranchers and also several that are of interest to people who raise horses.

Other sources of information for prospects for farms that primarily raise livestock might include a livestock association, if you have one. Another source of prospects would be the various auction houses. If there is a livestock market in your area, be sure to call on these people because they will certainly know the names of a number of people who are interested in large scale livestock raising. The same thing would be true of hogs or sheep.

As for horse farms, there are a number of different types of horses. For any type, there are usually horse auctions and if any of these are held in your locality, the people who conduct these auctions would be a good source of prospects. If there are any horse shows or county or state fairs at which there are show horses, you can frequently obtain a number of prospects from the managers of these shows or fairs. The business manager of the fair or horse show will often let you put an ad on the bulletin board in his office. These bulletins will be read by people interested in raising horses and might be a good source of prospects for you. The same thing can be done in auction houses where cattle or sheep are auctioned.

POINTS TO KEEP IN MIND

- In order to rent homes successfully, you must get to know what people look for in rental property.
- The next important thing to know is all of the details about the property that you have to offer. Know also the advantage of the location and the best use of the property.
- Know where to locate people who would be interested in the type of property which you have to offer.

Chapter 5

Apartments: The Biggest Gold Mine of Them All!

The leasing of apartments is one of the biggest real estate fields. There are millions of apartment units in the United States and in virtually every area of the country. It is not known what percentage of people live in apartments, but it must be large. In spite of the fact that more people live in their own single family homes today than ever before, there is still a very high percentage living in apartments.

The boom in building apartments in recent years in America has been phenomenal. This has been due to increasing population and the ease of obtaining mortgage money for new construction. Every section of the country has seen this boom in apartment building, and the units tend to become larger and larger. Many of these have been of the conventional type, but many of them represent new ideas in apartment living.

Many sections of the country have seen the construction of large numbers of high-rise apartments ranging from five to fifty stories in height. Many of these apartments are the very latest word in modern living, with wall-to-wall carpeting, air conditioning and other modern features. There has also been a great increase in cooperative and condominium apartments which represent another field of real estate, since the apartments are sold rather than rented.

Another recent development has been the garden apartment, where the amount of land area per apartment is much larger than in the case of the high-rise. The garden type seldom exceeds two stories in height and has parking space arranged so that each renter can park his car near his particular apartment. Many of these places have swimming pools and recreation rooms.

Another development has been the townhouse apartment, which usually consists of two stories with each apartment on two levels and with both the front and back walls facing the outside. A feature of the town house is the enclosed patio in the back so that each apartment owner has his own private little back yard. In this type of apartment, the corner apartments have only one common wall with other apartments, and those in the middle have only two.

A very large number of duplexes have also been constructed. These have been built for private individuals who usually purchase them from the builder, live in one of them and rent out the other. The theory behind the duplex is that it gives the person a home as well as an income from the other apartment.

From the standpoint of making money in leasing apartments, the biggest development is, of course, the best. Leasing a two or three hundred unit apartment can be put on a mass production basis, and profits can be high. The lease form itself would be uniform and the apartments themselves pretty much the same, and once the large development starts leasing, it usually fills up very rapidly, making a tidy income.

WHAT PEOPLE WANT IN APARTMENTS

When going into an apartment project, be sure to pick the ones that are the most attractive to renters. There are all kinds of people and they want different things, of course, but there are usually certain things in common that all people looking for apartments desire.

Convenience

The most obvious consideration, of course, is the value of the location. Is the apartment development located in a good neighborhood, and is it convenient to shopping centers, places of entertainment, schools and churches? Another element of convenience that is peculiar to apartment house living is the fact that the apartment renter has little responsibility for the maintenance of the property. Someone else looks after the property and if he wishes to be away, he knows that his apartment will be looked after while he is gone. For people who travel, this is a great convenience because when it becomes time to go somewhere, all they have to do is to close the door of the apartment and leave. When they come back, all that they have to do is to unlock the door and walk in. Someone has been looking after the property while they were away.

Another thing that provides convenience is the fact that in regard to any repairs or maintenance needed in the apartment, not only is someone else responsible for them, but the time of so doing can be arranged for the convenience of the apartment renter. If the family intends to be away on a trip, various repairs, such as new carpets or painting, can be done while they are away without any inconvenience.

Other conveniences that an apartment might have are coin-operated laundries and dry cleaning areas. These are usually found in large apartment developments. Also in even larger developments, there are frequently beauty parlors and barber shops, which are a great convenience to the people living in the apartments.

Flexibility

When a person owns his own home, he has made a large fixed investment. In the event that the character of the neighborhood changes, or for some reason or other he decides he does not like the location, there sometimes isn't anything he can do about it very soon. In apartment living, the leases generally do not exceed a year, and if the tenant finds he does not like the location or there is something about the apartment house he doesn't like, he can move very easily.

Frequently, after moving to a particular location in any neighborhood, the family may find the location inconvenient for them, or they may not like the neighbors or the policy of the management of the apartment house. Should these occur, it is comparatively easy for them to find another apartment somewhere else and move to it at the expiration of their lease. Many leases also have a clause providing that should the tenant wish to move out before the expiration of the lease, he can do so by paying one month's penalty rent.

It sometimes happens that a family finds it needs a larger apartment, and here again, the question of flexibility is of importance.

Low Investment

Another advantage of living in apartments is the fact that the capital investment required of the tenant is at a minimum. If he buys a home at today's prices, the capital investment is very large and even in an era of easy credit, requires a fairly good amount of cash. There are many families, especially young people who are just starting out in life, who find it difficult to obtain this amount of cash investment. They can, however, move into an apartment with a relatively low investment. In fact, if the apartment is furnished, the cash investment is practically nil.

Most apartments today, especially the new and modern ones, are partially furnished anyway. As a rule, the cooking equipment and the refrigeration equipment are included in the rent. Sometimes the apartment also furnishes dish washers, and in some cases even automatic clothes washers and dryers.

After the original cash investment in moving into a home is made, it is an interesting question as to which is the most economical manner of living: whether in an apartment house as a tenant or in a home as an owner. There are two sides to this question, and you can hear it debated in many different ways. Usually the two come out about the same. However, it still remains that it is possible to move into an apartment house with very little cash outlay.

Ease of Living

In apartment houses, the apartments are smaller, as a rule, than homes, and for that reason there is less housekeeping required. In modern apartments this is especially true, because the apartments are designed to make the daily chores of the housewife as light as possible.

With small kitchens, especially all electric ones, the serving of meals becomes a much simpler task than in older properties. Since the apartment is redecorated from time to time, the cleaning job is not quite so severe as in the home. Also apartments often furnish cleaning service from time to time, the cost of which is included in the rent. Some apartments, of course, furnish maid service that comes every day and does virtually all of the work. This is particularly desirable in the case of bachelors or a couple who both work.

Ownership

Another thing for you to consider is ownership policy, for different owners have different policies regarding their properties. Some owners look on apartments as something on which to spend as little money as possible to receive the highest possible rent. This type of property becomes difficult to rent, especially after a year or two of operation. On the other hand, some owners take pride in their property and try to keep it in perfect repair and in an attractive appearance at all times.

Another matter of policy which the owner must decide involves restrictions. Should the apartment be restricted to adults only, and should the tenants be allowed to keep pets; these are important considerations and sometimes affect the rentability of the apartments.

Comforts

Since all of the modern apartments are constructed with many comforts built into them, these have become a feature of modern living and are very essential in having an apartment which is easily rented. The capital investment required of an owner for air conditioning, wall-to-wall carpeting, electric kitchens, automatic heat and the other things that go along with modern apartments comes to a large sum. However, in renting many modern apartments, these comforts are all furnished in the rent and require no capital outlay other than payment of the first month's rent. It is always an advantage if your apartment house has these modern comforts, and it is also helpful if it has a swimming pool and recreation room.

What you are selling when you lease any residential area is the convenience and comfort of living in that spot. Needless to say, the cost of such living is an important factor too. It is a very easy matter to compare rentals among apartments, and this you should certainly do. It isn't very often you find an apartment house out of line on rent, as the owner usually has a pretty good idea of what rental schedules are. However, be sure that the rental schedule is in line with other similar properties.

WHO WANTS APARTMENTS

In finding tenants for apartments, the most important thing is to know what kind of people you are looking for. There are all kinds of people that are interested in finding apartment space, but these people can be classified into three general groups. It is helpful to know what people are in these groups and specifically why they want apartment space.

Older People

There are many older people who have always lived in apartments, like that type of living and wish to continue doing so. If these people are looking for apartments, it is generally because they want to change locations or think they can find a better and more modern place in which to live. These people generally know exactly what size of apartment they want, where they want it located and how much they are willing to pay.

Other older people who are seeking apartments are doing so because they find it increasingly burdensome to care for a single family home. These people may have raised a family, their children have left home and now there are only the two of them in a large house. It becomes burdensome to care for the large property, especially since only part of it is actually used, and the people caring for it are older and do not have the necessary energy. By having an apartment they not only cut down on housekeeping, but also do not have to be worried by the various repairs and maintenance work involved, since this is the responsibility of the owner or manager of the apartment. This is a prime reason why older people frequently give up single family homes and move into apartments.

These people are primarily interested in finding something barely large enough for their needs, so that the work of taking care of it will be at a minimum. They are also interested in convenient locations where they will be near shopping centers and on convenient streets. They want a place where it will be easy for their children to visit them as well as for delivery people to find. They also want something that is convenient to medical services and hospitals and in a location that their doctor can easily find in the event they need him.

Moving Closer in

Sometimes older people decide to live in apartments because they can have a home closer to the center of the city. Frequently these people, when raising a family, live in the suburbs and enjoy suburban living very much. When their family is grown and has left home, they are more interested in convenience. Over a period of time, there is a lot of driving covering a great many miles going back and forth from a suburban location to the facilities offered by the downtown area. By getting an apartment close to the city, this driving effort is greatly reduced. Also they will generally find that public transportation to their apartment location is available, so they will not need to drive a car at all.

Many of these people want to be assured of better police and fire protection. It is also frequently desirable to be near office buildings and theatres which they can easily reach from a downtown location, whereas they would be a long distance removed from the suburban one.

Greater Freedom

Another reason for older people moving to an apartment is that they have greater freedom of movement. If they have a large home which they have to take care of, it is difficult to get away for a week or two to visit with children or friends. In an apartment, however, since someone else is responsible for looking after the property, they can leave at any time. Frequently these people, having retired and no longer active in business, have sufficient money to travel and like to be away from home quite a bit. Living in an apartment permits much greater freedom and enables them to get away whenever they wish, without being worried about what is happening to their home while they are gone.

On the other side of the coin, of course, is the fact that in their own home they have lots of room for their children and friends to visit them. However it is easily possible today to find an apartment which has a spare bedroom and which is large enough to accommodate company. In owning their own home, there are constantly things arising that make it difficult for them to get away. Perhaps the property needs some repair and it is necessary for them to be there while the repair man is there. In an apartment it is not necessary for them to worry about any of this, since repairs and necessary maintenance can be effected during their absence. There is also the matter of insurance. Insurance rates on a house that is left vacant for any length of time are greatly increased. Of course, there would be no insurance increase in the matter of apartments.

Young People

Probably the biggest reason why newly married couples and other young people live in an apartment is the difficulty of obtaining the cash down payment with which to start a home of their own. In having a home of their own, there is not only the down payment on the property itself to consider, but the cost of furnishing it. They can rent an apartment already furnished or if unfurnished, the cost of furnishing an apartment is much less than that of a home. Since in an apartment generally the cooking and refrigeration equipment is furnished, there are two expensive items that they do not have to buy. Also the apartment will be smaller than the average house, and for that reason also will require less in the way of furnishings.

Young people will usually find that in renting an apartment, they can obtain certain luxuries that would be completely beyond their means if they bought their own home. Such things as air conditioning, central heat, a swimming pool, recreation rooms and other comforts would be completely beyond their means if they built a home of their own. However, they can obtain these things in a modern apartment by paying one month's rent in advance.

Another reason why young people like apartment living is the fact that in so many families, both of them work. There is a decided tendency at present for the man and wife to both be employed in full-time jobs. They may work different hours in different locations, and it is much more convenient to go to and from the apartment than it would be from a home of their own. There is also the matter of housekeeping. Where both members of the family are employed full time, it is difficult to find the necessary time to take care of a home with the necessary housekeeping work that would be involved. However, it is much simpler in an apartment, and in fact many such couples rent apartments that have maid service.

Near Other People

Another reason why young people rent apartments is that they like to live near other people. Especially if one works and one does not, the one that is left at home might feel very isolated and lonely in a home of their own. However, in an apartment there are nearby neighbors with whom acquaintance can be made, and since there are always people around there would be no reason for the one left at home to feel lonely.

Temporary in Area

There are certain people who do not expect to stay in one spot very long. For that reason it is difficult for them to decide to buy a home and make an investment which might be frozen for a good number of years. These people are therefore, of necessity, interested in finding an apartment.

Some of these people are young people who are working for large corporations and know that they are going to be transferred every few years from one area of the country to another. A lot of large corporations have the definite policy of never leaving certain of their employees in one place for very long. There is also the matter of promotion. Frequently an employee is offered a promotion that might require him to move to another city. His movements and his progress in the company could be much more flexible by having an apartment, rather than being tied down to one city by the large investment in a home.

There are also many people who are involved in training programs. They may be a trainee for a large corporation knowing that as soon as their training period is completed, they will be transferred somewhere else. This training period may involve more than one location. They may be assured that during the training period they will have to move three or four times. For that reason, they are only interested in renting space, not in buying it.

Another group that is interested in apartment space would be people attending school. There are a lot of married couples, one or both of whom are attending college. They do not expect to be in that locality after graduation, and for that reason are looking for temporary space. These people are interested in a one- to four-year lease, but no longer than that.

There are also people doing survey work who are sent by large surveying organizations that do research work in a locality. They know that as soon as the job is completed, they will be moving again.

HOW TO REACH APARTMENT PROSPECTS

Essentially, reaching prospective tenants for apartment spaces is about the same as seeking tenants for homes or estates. There is some difference in that usually the rentals will be smaller, your profit per lease smaller and you won't be able to afford to spend quite as much money per accomplished lease. For that reason, you have more of a shotgun approach to apartment renting than to homes and estates.

Advertising

Probably your most effective medium of advertising is a sign on the apartment house property itself. This sign should be clearly visible from the street. You should be careful to have a minimum of words on it so that traffic moving by can read your message. The important idea to convey includes the words *For Rent* and your name and telephone number. If these stand out, you will get the essentials of your message across.

It would be a good idea to have these signs painted in contrasting colors so your message will be easily read. Suggested copy for this would be:

> *Modern Apartment, Now Leasing,* your name, address and phone number.

If, in your business, you maintain signs on highways leading into town, at least some space on these signs could be devoted to your leasing activities. Possibly the words *Homes* and *Apartments for Rent* would take care of that situation. Then people coming into town for the first time or moving there who see your sign will look you up.

As far as advertising in newspapers is concerned, it is probably over a period of time most advantageous to have an institutional type of ad. This could be in the classified section of the paper under "Apartments for Rent," but would not specify any certain or definite property. A very brief ad mentioning that you are specializing in apartment rentals will have a cumulative effect, if left in long enough. If your business is sizable in apartment renting, it might pay you to leave this ad in all of the time.

A sample ad might read as follows:

Apartments for Rent. Efficiencies, one, two and three bedroom. Furnished or unfurnished. Contact us for the best choice in town. Name, address and phone number.

If you do have a large apartment development, it might pay you to place a display ad about this. If there is enough money involved, you could have an open house on a Sunday and advertise a model apartment in the papers. Then when people come to see the model apartment advertised, you can get their names and addresses and perhaps close several leases.

Recently, on a new apartment building just started here in our city, the first apartment finished was made a model apartment, and the open house was held. In a period of about three days, every apartment in the project was rented before the building was actually completed.

Obtaining Prospects from Other People

As in any other phase of real estate work, the more people you know, the more prospects you will get. People with whom you become acquainted through clubs or churches are excellent sources of prospects, especially if they learn that you have rental properties. This sort of thing has a cumulative effect as word-of-mouth advertising takes a long time, but is good for the long pull.

Other sources of prospects are, of course, your Chamber of Commerce, large industrial concerns in your area, banks, schools and, of course, brokers. If you are specializing in leases, you can obtain many leads from other people who are in the real estate business.

POINTS TO KEEP IN MIND

- *Know what people want.* There are certain advantages of apartment house living over any other type, and you should be familiar with all of such advantages.
- *Know what type of people live in apartments.* In this way you will know how to advertise, where to find prospects and how to talk to them.
- *Know how to advertise apartments.* You must reach the largest number of prospects, so word your advertisements so that they will arouse interest on the part of the reader with as few words as possible.

Chapter 6

Money-Making Secrets of Leasing Office Buildings and Office Space

One of the largest fields in leasing is represented by office space. There are millions of offices of all kinds, including insurance companies, real estate offices and professional offices. Leasing of these can be a very profitable business. How profitable it will be depends to a large extent on the type of contract you obtain from the owner and the type of property that you have for lease.

TYPES OF LISTING CONTRACTS

The important thing in listing office space for lease is to tie up an entire office building. An occasional lease on small space hardly justifies your time, but if you have control of an entire building, the larger the better, you have a much better chance of making significant profit out of your leasing operations. The important thing is to get exclusive contracts.

Leasing Contract Only

The simplest form of contract is one in which you have no other duty except to find tenants for the office space. In this type of contract you have no responsibility at all for any maintenance of the building, collecting of rents or any other duties. This is not a usual contract for office buildings because it is sometimes difficult to tell exactly where the duties of a leasing agent end and the duties of a building superintendent begin.

A disadvantage of this type of contract is the fact that you must consult the owners on every lease that you make. It is necessary to consult them about the size of space that you are planning to lease and submit to them information about the prospective tenant. Sometimes it is difficult to get in touch with the owners of the office building. In the event the building is owned by a large corporation, it is necessary to contact someone who has authority to make leases, and sometimes this is not as easy as it sounds. Frequently owners of office buildings are absentee owners who do not even live in the city where the building is located. This means that you are constantly delayed in making leases and constantly put to extra trouble in trying to arrange meetings with the owners to determine whether or not a specific lease should be made.

The advantage of this type of lease, of course, is that you do not waste much time because your only duty is to obtain tenants. Of course, the rate of commission in this case is less than it would be if you were to assume other duties, but it is probably more profitable in relation to the time spent. When you are acting as leasing agent only, you do not have to be available all of the time as you would in other types of contracts, and you would not have to maintain an office force as would generally otherwise be the case.

Leasing and Management Contracts

Most contracts regarding office buildings combine the functions of leasing offices and managing the office building. The two functions go hand in hand, and usually the agent in this case has authority to make leases without consulting anyone. This type of contract necessitates that either you be available practically all the time or have someone who is available. If the office building is large enough to justify it, you might have an office in the building with a secretary who is there during office hours.

Under this type of contract tenants will be calling you when anything is needed in their offices. Usually a list of repairmen is kept who can be called whenever it becomes necessary. Your office would be responsible for maintenance of the property, such as seeing that light bulbs, etc. are in good condition.

In a contract of this kind, the commission rates are much higher than one in which you only act as leasing agent. Another advantage of this type of contract is the fact that you do not have to waste time consulting the owners, and you can make decisions on your own. It is also easier for you to make decisions since you have better control over possible changes in office space. If you have a prospective tenant who wants a larger space than you have immediately available, you can decide yourself whether or not it is feasible to make suitable alterations.

Under this type of contract, you will also be responsible for collecting the rents. If you exercise due discretion in leasing space and if your building is a desirable and modern one, you can pick and choose tenants and take only those whom you feel will pay the rent promptly without any effort on your part. It is also necessary that you keep records on the property since your office would be responsible for all items of income and outgo. On a large property this requires quite a lot of bookkeeping. You can have a system installed by an accountant who is familiar with this type of operation and assign one person on your staff to take care of these records. A report is made to the owners of the property at periodic intervals, usually each month. All receipts are deposited in the bank and all disbursements are made by check. This simplifies the records and gives the owners a better check on the operation of the building. If you plan to enter into this type of contract, be sure that you choose a good, well-located and desirable building, so that the operation will be profitable to you. If you have one type of contract like this and the operation is successful, you will find that other people come to you to get you to manage their office buildings. There is quite a demand for office building management.

WHAT PEOPLE WANT IN OFFICE SPACE

If you make an exclusive contract to lease or manage, or you own an office building and it is old and out of date and not too desirable for tenants, you will find that the operation will not be profitable to you. It will take so much of your time trying to find tenants and so much time in caring for maintenance and repairs and other activities, that you will not justify your time with the commissions or profits earned. There are many aspects that enter into the desirability of office buildings.

Location

The considerations of primary importance in choosing a location are the access to it and type of neighborhood. It should be situated so that it is easy to reach by car or, in very large cities, by public transportation.

The neighborhood is also of much importance because both employees and customers like to be in pleasant surroundings. If the building is in a bad neighborhood, it will not be a successful office building. It is very helpful to be located in an area where there are other modern and attractive buildings. The view from the windows of the office building should be pleasant and not depressing.

Modern Building

The building should be modern in that it presents a clean and neat appearance and has central heat and air conditioning. Air conditioning has become a requisite of successful office building operation.

Other features of modern buildings that are necessary today are fireproof construction, modern and easy to operate elevators that give rapid service from floor to floor. Also, the interior decorations of the offices should present a cheerful, clean and up-to-date appearance.

Maintenance

The day-to-day upkeep of the building is one of its most important features. Does the management furnish janitorial service? This is very important with most concerns.

Regardless of whether or not janitorial service is furnished within the offices themselves, the general upkeep of the building is of vital significance. Does the management keep the hallways clean, and does it keep the heating and air conditioning equipment in good condition? Are minor repairs which constantly become necessary in office buildings promptly attended to? Lighting and plumbing always need minor repairs. There isn't anything more annoying to a tenant than to find that the building management is dilatory about making necessary maintenance work. Usually they look around the building to see how clean it is maintained, and this look will answer the management question very quickly.

Parking

Of course, an essential nowadays in any office building is convenience of parking. In outlying neighborhoods, most office buildings have their own parking lots. In downtown areas, there must be parking garages or parking lots nearby. This is of importance not only for customers but for employees that work in the office building.

WHO WANTS OFFICE SPACE

In general there are two types of offices. One type uses office space only for its own employees, and the other is the type that has many visits from customers or from the public. The needs of these two types are somewhat different.

Those Who Do Not Have Public Callers

This category of office space users covers a number of different kinds of offices. In this type, the space is used by employees who work within the office, and there is no need for anyone other than these employees to enter the area.

One of the largest categories of this type of office space is the district office. Many concerns have district sales offices where they have sales meetings with their sales force and where the clerical work in connection with sales campaigns are kept. Frequently they are also district accounting and record keeping offices. These offices do not have any outside visitors except possibly supervisory personnel from other offices or from the main office of the company.

Other types of offices that exist only for the convenience of the employees are trade associations of various kinds where the records of such associations are kept but where the members of the association seldom visit. In any sizable city you will find a number of these listed in the telephone book.

One of the largest types of offices to be found in this category includes various government offices. There are a large number of federal and state offices that have very few visitors from the public. Frequently these agencies of the government have their own office buildings, but frequently they need other space as well. There are, of course, many government offices that do have visitors, and the requirements of these are a little different.

Other types of offices that do not have many public visitors are credit agencies, telephone answering services, adjustors, etc. Regardless of the particular type of business involved, these offices all have about the same requirements.

One of the first requirements is, as is the case in all office buildings, pleasant surroundings. Employee morale is dependent to a large extent on the way the office building looks, the neighborhood it is in and how convenient it is for them to reach it. Another thing that is necessary is ample parking for the number of employees that work in the building. Frequently this type of office will be located in outlying areas where the building has its own parking lot. This is obviously very desirable.

Another important aspect is adequate lighting. Since most of the work is of a close nature, such as bookkeeping, drafting or engineering work, it is necessary that the lighting be so arranged as to be adequate for the purpose for which it is needed. Frequently it is necessary to put in new lights in order to make the office suitable for the purpose for which it is needed.

Other necessary conveniences are nearby restaurants. Frequently each office will have its own little snack bar where the employees can make coffee and sandwiches.

Of course, one outstanding need for offices of this type is convenient arrangement. This is usually a matter to be worked out by the tenant and will frequently require removal of partitions or inserting additional ones. Since the work is of an office nature, each company has its own needs and ideas and is usually arranged to suit the tenant.

Those Offices That Do Have Public Callers

This type of office is the most numerous. There are real estate offices, travel agencies, mortgage loan companies and many others. One of the largest groups, of course, are professional people such as doctors, dentists, accountants, etc. There are also a number of brokerage businesses of various kinds that require office space for their customers.

It is important for offices of this kind to be even more easy of access than offices which do not have public visitors. Also there must be additional parking to take care of the visitors that these offices will have.

It is also important that these offices be large enough. Too frequently firms of this kind rent small office space and find that it is very inconvenient for them and for their customers. There should be an ample waiting room to take care of the heaviest possible load of visitors that may be expected.

Arrangement of these offices is also important, especially where cashier's windows or private interview rooms are needed. Usually this arrangement must be different for each type of firm and will have to be tailor-made to the tenant.

Certain types of offices, of course, do have special needs. Usually an attorney will want his offices located so that it is convenient to the courthouse. Doctors like their offices to be convenient to the hospitals. This saves them time traveling back and forth as they sometimes will have to make many trips each day. These special needs will have to be determined on an individual basis with each tenant.

HOW TO REACH PROSPECTIVE TENANTS

Once you know what you have to offer, you can easily determine what type of tenants are your best prospects.

Display Advertisements

If you have a large office building, it will pay you to place a display ad in the newspaper when your building is ready for occupancy. Usually this advertisement should be put in the paper a month or so in advance of the time when your building will be completed. This is so that you can begin to take applications. People who are in other and older buildings will want to move into your newer one and will need to reserve office space before their lease expires on their present location. The most effective type of display ad would be one in which a picture of the building is shown. Usually the best place in the paper for this is near the financial pages.

Direct Mail

You can get a mailing list of prospective tenants from several sources. One of the best of these is the telephone directory of your city. You can go through the Yellow Pages of this directory and pick out the type of businesses you feel would be interested in your particular building. You can then send a form letter to these people inviting them to look over the facilities in the building for which you are agent. Frequently noticing the addresses in the telephone directory will enable you to leave out certain names that you do not think would be interested in moving.

Other sources of mailing lists are directories of tenants in other office buildings. Some of the least attractive and oldest office buildings have tenants who would like to move, if they knew of a good place to which to move. By making a list of the tenants that are found on the building directory, you will have a very good list of names from which to make your mailing list.

The letter itself should be as brief as possible and yet give the primary reasons why you think your office space is desirable. The outstanding features are, of course, location, parking, flexible arrangement of offices and the fact that your building is new and modern. A sample letter that should get good results is Exhibit 6-1.

Dear Sir:

Wouldn't you like to have a beautifully decorated office in a new and modern building with ample parking space, elevator service, and air conditioning?

Our new building will be ready for occupancy in about thirty days. See us now so you can choose the location you like best.

Very truly yours,

Letter to Prospective Tenant

Exhibit 6-1

Telephone Solicitations

Telephones are best used as follow-ups. If you get an answer to any of your mailing or to any of your ads, you can follow the inquiry up by telephone.

Frequently you can go over your list of names, pick out the concerns that you think would need the largest office space and follow up a mailing by calling them, even though you have not yet received an inquiry from them. It is well worth your time to work by telephone with the tenants that you think would be large and desirable ones. Your source of names for this would be the same as for the direct mailings; that is, telephone directories and office building directories.

POINTS TO KEEP IN MIND

- The larger the building, the better the profit return.
- Know what people who are looking for office space want.
- Know who needs office space.
- Your prospects can be reached by newspaper, direct mail or telephone solicitation.

Chapter 7

How to Cash In on the Coming Boom in Warehouse Leasing

In recent years, there has been a wide-spread shortage of warehouse space. Due to the tremendous business expansion of the last decade, existing warehouse facilities were soon all put to use and much more was needed. Warehouse space is a big business – and a good one.

LISTING WAREHOUSE SPACE

As a general principle, the larger the proposition the more profitable it will be for you. Too many people waste too much time working on small properties which, even if they are successful in leasing, do not result in enough profit to make the work and expense worthwhile. Another thing that must be kept in mind is to have desirable properties that can be leased with a minimum of time and effort.

Transportation Factor

Since, in the very nature of the warehouse business, many tons of material and supplies are constantly moved in and out, location relative to transportation facilities is essential. Some warehouse operations are conducted exclusively by truck. In these situations, the highway availability is important. If the transportation by truck involves long distances, the location must be near interstate highways with good access to them. Long haul trucking routes invariably use the interstate highways due to the savings in time and expense of operation of the truck.

Some warehouse operations transport primarily by rail. This is the case where commodities are very bulky or very heavy in proportion to their value. In this case, the warehouse would need a railroad siding which can be serviced by one of the leading railroads. How long the siding must be depends on the number of car loads of freight used by the facility. In some facilities, where a lot of freight comes in and out, the siding should be long enough to accommodate several freight cars. Along with this, loading platforms of sufficient height and strength must be available. For facilities which use primarily truck hauling, there should be several loading platforms and several entrances into and from the warehouse.

Construction

Warehouses are usually simple in their construction. Fundamentally, it is just a large room with very few pillars or other obstructions to interfere with the free movement of freight. Generally, these buildings are built of concrete block with a concrete floor. It is important that the floor be strong enough to bear heavy loads. This is known as the load factor, and the heavier the load that can be sustained by the floor, the more different types of businesses that can use that warehouse. Sometimes merchandise or the supplies stored in warehouses are extremely heavy; this is especially true of paint and metal products.

Generally speaking, a warehouse operation does not require as much heat in the wintertime as in other types of structures. It must only be kept warm enough to be comfortable for the employees. There is seldom any attempt to air-condition such a structure.

Zoning

In nearly all areas, the zoning of the land upon which the warehouse is built is essential. Most localities have several types of industrial zoning, and one or more of them will cover warehouse operations. In most places the industrial zoning which permits warehouses is in areas convenient to highways and railroad sidings. In fact, most of the warehouses will be found in industrial areas in or near good roads and railroads.

New Buildings

One of the best sources of obtaining business for renting warehouse space is in connection with new buildings that are built to suit a particular tenant. In this case, what you need is good land, which, of course, must be zoned properly and on which a warehouse can be built to suit a tenant on a long-term lease. These buildings can be built in very short order and can be constructed according to specifications and requirements of a particular tenant.

Due to the fact that so many large firms have differing requirements as to what they need in size and construction of warehouse space, it is frequently much easier to have a building built for them than to find one already erected. These leases must be made for a long term of years, so that the owner of the building can amortize it over the period of the lease. These buildings generally have a low cost per square foot and the rental, of course, is low in proportion. However, since some of these warehouses are extremely large, the rental can run into high figures.

WHO WANTS WAREHOUSE SPACE

In order for you to find tenants for warehouse space, it is necessary to know where to look. There is a tremendous demand for warehouse space all over the United States from many different types of concerns.

Manufacturing Plants

Often, especially in a period of expanding business, manufacturing plants will find they have insufficient space in which to store raw materials. Sometimes these companies will stockpile materials in anticipation of a coming shortage, and this takes space. Also, frequently the business of the manufacturer will exceed his expectations and he will have to work two or three shifts instead of one, and consequently needs more space for storing materials which he uses in his manufacturing process.

Another thing which many manufacturing plants need is additional space for various types of supplies. These would be parts which are frequently replaced on their machinery or materials which are used up in the process of manufacturing.

Recently we were trying to lease an old, rather out-of-date warehouse with 50,000 square feet. We contacted the president of a manufacturing concern in our city, and it developed that they needed extra storage space very badly.

The size of the warehouse was about right for them, but it did need a lot of upgrading. A long-term lease was arranged, based on the landlord's remodeling the building to suit the tenant, and a very satisfactory arrangement was made. The profit to the owner of the building was sizable, and his income from it continues for at least fifteen years, which was the primary term of the lease.

Due to the size of the contract and the length of the lease, the real estate commission amounted to over $10,000 – a very handsome profit for the broker involved.

Distribution Warehouses

The largest use for warehouses is generally found in various types of wholesale distribution. It can be for such widely diversified things as meat, hosiery, automobile tires, food items, and almost anything else. Generally speaking, the reason for this is that the goods or commodities are distributed to customers in comparatively small amounts. For firms which operate nationally, small shipments are very expensive, especially on long hauls. For this reason, they maintain a number of warehouses in various areas of the country. They can ship to one of these warehouses in large quantities, by carload or truckload lots and distribute them out of the warehouse in smaller quantities to their customers.

Special Use Warehouses

Many of these distribution firms require exceptional construction or arrangement for the warehouse space they use. This would be especially true of meat packing companies, that require cold rooms and insulated walls, of course, in order to maintain the required temperature. This would also be true of frozen food companies that distribute all types of frozen food in your area.

Paint is a very heavy item, and the important feature in a warehouse for something of this nature is the load factor of the floor and the ease with which the merchandise can be moved from one part of the warehouse to the other by mechanical means.

Interior Arrangement of the Warehouse

Usually the interior arrangement of the warehouse presents no problems, since it is fundamentally just an open room. However, some operations require office space, and it is necessary to have a few rooms partitioned off for that purpose. The loading docks, whether for trucks or railroad cars, should be so arranged that aisles can run directly from them to any part of the warehouse. Most warehouse operations today use mechanized equipment such as fork lifts and require easy access to all parts of the building. The doors on warehouses, of course, should be very wide to permit easy ingress and exit.

Wholesale Businesses

Wholesale businesses are very large users of warehouse space, and there are many wholesale grocers, hardware companies, etc., that need warehouse space constantly. Some of these companies will have thousands of customers in an area of possibly two hundred square miles, and they will need a warehouse from which to distribute to these various customers and fill the orders that are received from them.

These wholesale operations exist in almost all types of businesses, especially those that run into high volume, but comparatively small individual items. An item such as furniture is large enough, usually, that it can be distributed directly from the factory. However, on smaller items such does not work satisfactorily. This is especially true where a number of different items are made in one shipment to one customer. An example might be a wholesale hardware company where one customer might order a few gallons of paint, a dozen tools and a number of other items. In this case a warehouse from which to assemble these items into one container is very essential. Due to the transportation expense, the warehouse should be located as near as possible to the customers and this is the reason why wholesale concerns, as a rule, have a number of warehouses in different parts of the area which they serve.

SELLING WAREHOUSE LEASES

Since there is a shortage of warehouse space and a great demand for it on the part of all types of concerns, it is not difficult to sell warehouse leases. The primary requirement is to have the space available. Since industrial and wholesale firms are actively looking for space, it is important to have the space available for them and to let it be known that you are specializing in handling all types of leases.

Your Stock in Trade

In any phase of the real estate business, your stock in trade or merchandise consists of the properties that you have available. This is especially true in the warehouse leasing business, since your succes will largely depend on how many different properties it is possible for you to offer prospective tenants.

Since there is such a great variety of concerns looking for warehouse space, you should acquire as great a variety of warehouse spaces as possible. You should also get just as much properly zoned land as you can, as one of the largest fields for you will be building to suit the tenants that you obtain.

Advertising

The main goal that you should try to accomplish by advertising is to become known as a specialist in handling leases. If you can convey this idea adequately in your community, the concerns that are looking for space will come to you rather than making it necessary for you to seek them. Probably the best form of advertising for this purpose is the use of signs.

You should have a uniform sign with an attractive color scheme and an attractive shape. It is important that this sign be uniform, so that people in your area will begin to think of you the minute they see the sign. It creates a trademark which establishes in people's minds that you are a specialist in leasing. The best place to put these signs is on properties which you are offering for lease.

Most of the companies that are looking for warehouse space have employees that are responsible for finding it, and these employees will usually get zoning maps, find out where the proper zoning is in the community and then ride around those areas to see what they can find. If on their rounds they see a number of your signs, they very soon learn that you are the person to talk to about leasing warehouse space.

If you really go into the leasing business on a big scale and become a specialist in it, it would probably pay to have large signs on the main highways leading into your community. These signs would not be restricted to advertising warehouse space, but simply to establishing the fact that you are specializing in all types of leases. On all signs, of course, you must convey the message that you are a specialist in handling leases as well as your name and phone number, so that there will be no problem in getting in touch witih you. These signs should be designed so that they can be read from a moving vehicle and for that reason, should not be cluttered up with too much copy.

Personal Contact

One of the quickest ways to become known as a leasing specialist in your area is through personal contact. If you tell each person you talk to about your business, the word-of-mouth advertising will be very valuable, since the message will gradually spread from one person to another.

Some people are in the position to give you leads as to who is interested in finding warehouse space. There are many people who are in touch with various industrial and wholesale concerns and can refer these people to you.

Some of the most important people for you to know and be in personal contact with would include the manager of the local Chamber of Commerce, your banker, the president of the local Junior Chamber of Commerce chapter, and people who are leaders in the various luncheon clubs. It would pay you to belong to the Chamber of Commerce and to a good luncheon club, such as the Rotary, Kiwanis or Lions Club. In this way, you will get to know the businessmen in your community. These people know other people, and in this way word can soon get around that you are specializing in leasing. Since so many business people know about this, they can refer other people that they know to you.

POINTS TO KEEP IN MIND

- Be as flexible as possible in what you have to offer.
- Excellent deals are made by building a warehouse to suit a good tenant.
- In leasing warehouse space, personal contact is probably the best form of advertising you have.

Chapter 8

Lucrative Leasing of Space for Chain Store Branches

There is a difference between chain store branches and franchise stores. Chain store branches are owned and operated by the chain store company itself with their own employees. The franchise store is owned by the individual who operates it and who is operating under a franchise agreement with the principal chain store company. Sometimes it is difficult to tell whether any one particular store is a company operation or a franchise operation, as sometimes they look exactly alike. The important thing from the real estate broker's standpoint is to find out who signs the lease. The chain store branches' leases are usually signed by the chain store company itself. This is usually a large financially strong company, and their signature makes the lease a very strong one.

Sometimes the franchise store leases are signed by the owner of the store only. Other companies have the policy of cosigning or guaranteeing their franchise store leases. In this case usually the lease will be signed by the owner of the store with a separate agreement at the bottom of the lease, or sometimes in a separate instrument, that the chain store company will pay the rent in the event of a default by the owner of the franchise store. The importance of this signature is the fact that the owner of the property can negotiate a mortgage loan on the building to a much greater advantage to himself if the lease is guaranteed by the large concern. Most lending institutions feel that a lease guaranteed by a triple "A" company is one of the best securities they can possibly have.

TYPES OF CHAIN STORES AND WHAT THEY WANT

There are many types of chain stores that are expanding rapidly. They are constantly looking for locations for branch stores in various parts of the United States. Some of these are national chains that are concerned with finding locations in all fifty states. Others are more regional chains that cover four or five states, and some of them are local outfits that have all of their stores in one particular state.

Supermarkets

There are several retail grocery companies who operate on a national scale. Most of these companies are constantly expanding the number of their stores and are always on the lookout for locations. There are a still greater number of similar companies that operate on a regional basis, in that while they have a great many stores, they do not operate in all states. There are also some very good local outfits that have from ten to forty stores in one locality.

These companies usually require a store building of from 8,000 square feet up to 25,000 or 30,000 depending on the size of the market they expect to serve. They will make a survey of any area in which they think they might have a possible interest, and as a result of the survey can pretty well determine what the potential of the store in that location will be.

These concerns require locations that are near many people and which have easy access and ample parking. The requirement on parking is that there be three square feet of parking area or more to each square foot of building. If they decide the location requires a 12,000 square foot store, they will need an area of at least 48,000 square feet overall. Most of this type of store has moved to the suburban areas and is seldom to be found in the downtown districts. These concerns almost always prefer that the owner of the property construct a building for them on a long-term lease. Most of them will give a lease of at least fifteen years. The building has to be built to their specifications. They will usually pay a rental based on a percentage of sales or a fixed amount, whichever is greater. The usual percentage runs between 1 and 2 percent, and the fixed amount of rent will vary anywhere from $1.35 per square foot up to about $1.85.

One of the best supermarket deals that we made recently involved a national chain that had several stores in our market area, but there was one part of the market which was not being served by this particular company. Noticing this, we tried to find a location that might be of interest to them in that particular area of the city. The amount of space necessary, about an acre, is a large lot and there are not too many of them, so it was very easy to narrow the matter down to two or three locations and then choose the best of these. The chain was then contacted through their real estate department in their regional office. The information as to the name of the manager of that real estate department and location of his office was obtained through the local manager of one of their stores in our area.

We sent a map of the city showing the location we had in mind to the real estate manager. It was of immediate interest to him, and he liked it. It takes considerable time to effect a final lease with a large chain store concern, but this one went through very well and was based on a 13,500 square foot store on a fifteen year lease with a guaranteed minimum rental of $1.50 per square foot or a 1¼ percentage of sales, whichever was higher. Due to the strength of the tenant and the terms of the lease, it was possible for the owner of the property to obtain a loan sufficient to cover all of the cost of construction and part of the cost of the land. It made a profitable return on the investment and over the period of the lease will add considerably to the estate of the property owner.

On a deal of this kind, the real estate commission to the broker is approximately $1,000 per year for fifteen years, so you can see that it is very profitable from the broker's standpoint as well as from the viewpoint of the owner of the property.

Restaurants

There are a number of different types of restaurants that are expanding the number of their units. Generally these can be classified as drive-in restaurants where curb service is given and other restaurants where there is no curb service but where dining is on the inside of the building only. There are also combinations of these two types with both curb service and inside dining. There are a number of specialty restaurants that deal in some particular kind of food, such as pancake houses, donut houses, steak houses, etc.

Probably the majority of these various restaurant chains operate on a franchise basis. Some of them will guarantee the lease and others will not. Generally these leases are good ones if the chain is a successful one and enjoys considerable good will on the part of the public.

The drive-in restaurants and others that cater to the motoring public do need ample parking area and a location where it is easy to get in and out. The preferred location for this type of restaurant is usually one that is on a through highway and also in a residential area. If the restaurant can be close to a college or university, that is also favorable. Most of these chains prefer for the owner of the land to build and lease to them, although sometimes they will buy locations and build their own building. It is very rare for any of these firms to lease land on a long-term basis and construct their building on the leased land. This, however, sometimes happens.

There are a number of other types of restaurant operations. There are chains which specialize in operating restaurants in institutions such as hospitals and colleges, etc. Another specialty type that is quite popular in many parts of the country is the cafeteria. These companies rely on a very large volume of food business in order to make a profit, and they must be in an area where they can feed people by the thousands for at least two meals a day, lunch and dinner. These buildings are quite expensive to build, and for that reason the rent is usually higher than in most other types of restaurants.

Generally speaking from the broker's, owner's or investor's standpoint in making a lease, it is important to get a sales percentage in the rental terms. By sales percentage I mean that the concern will pay a certain percentage of their sales or a minimum guaranteed rental, whichever is greater. The usual percentage used in many of these restaurants is 5 percent. In some cases it might be more than this depending on the type of facility.

Recently in our city we were contacted by the regional manager of a large supermarket chain to see if we could rent one of the buildings occupied by them. This particular unit of the chain was not profitable and they wished to close the store, but they were involved in a long-term lease. It seemed to us a good location for a drive-in restaurant, and we contacted the president of a large firm. As it turned out, this firm was not only looking for a restaurant location, but also a location for a commissary. They liked the location of the supermarket very much. A meeting was arranged with the owners of the property and the officials of the drive-in restaurant concern. The drive-in restaurant was willing to make a lease based on 5 percent of their sales or a fixed minimum rental which amounted to about $2.00 per square foot per year, and this lease was more advantageous to the landlord than the one which he had with the supermarket. It was enough better than the supermarket lease to justify the landlord's making extensive alterations to the building. A deal was made, the supermarket was relieved of their liabilities under the lease and a new and better lease was made between the landlord and the drive-in restaurant. This was a very profitable proposition for everybody concerned as the owner got a higher return on his property, the restaurant chain obtained an excellent location that they wanted for one of their restaurants and their commissary, and the supermarket was relieved from paying rent on an unprofitable store.

Dry Cleaners

Everyone is familiar with the tremendous growth in the number of dry cleaning stores in existence. Usually these are of the quick service variety, the one-hour cleaners, four-hour cleaners, and so forth. One of the usual requirements is a drive-in window. For that reason the location has to be such that a drive-in window is possible with traffic coming in from one direction and going out another.

Most of these installations are owned by the individuals who operate them. Sometimes the manufacturer of the equipment used will guarantee some or all of the lease. This is very desirable if it can be done.

Recently we effected a lease with a company which has a chain of one-hour dry cleaners. Since the location was the only one suitable in an area of about twelve or fourteen blocks, the company was immediately interested in it. After writing the president of the concern and sending him a map of the city showing the location, we followed it up by a phone call and arranged an appointment for him to visit us and view the property. As a result of this, a lease was made for a period of fifteen years on a building to be built according to the specifications of the dry cleaning concern. This lease was based on 8 percent of their gross intake of $2.00 per square foot per year, whichever was greater. The owner of the property built the basic building, and the dry cleaning concern put in all of their own plumbing, wiring, boiler and so forth that it needed especially for their operation. Due to the fact that so much of the expensive part of the building was done by the tenant, the owner of the property is able to recover all of the cash that he invested in a period of only about two years. After that he has no investment in the property, the rental is paying off the mortgage which he would have free and clear in about eight or nine years and his estate will have a valuable piece of property at no cost to it.

Branch Banks

Practically all modern branch banks have drive-in windows. Unless the location you have in mind is suitable for a drive-in window, you are undoubtedly wasting your time by trying to make a deal with a bank. Another point to keep in mind in locating branch banks is the fact that their installations require unusual equipment, the biggest item of which is probably the vault. Some leases are made with the landowner constructing the building and the bank installing the vault at their own expense. Unless the lease is a very long one, it is a good idea to have a clause in the lease requiring the bank to take the vault out should they not renew their lease.

Drug Stores

Generally speaking there are two types of drug stores, one of which is primarily interested in prescription business and is usually known as a pharmacy. The other drug stores are much larger and carry a great variety of merchandise. Some of them are as big as twenty or twenty-five thousand square feet of floor area and are departmentalized much like a department store.

The pharmacy type of operation is usually interested in locations near hospitals or near medical buildings where there are a large number of doctors' offices.

The larger drug stores are interested in residential areas where there are many people and where their stores will be convenient and easy of access to these people.

The usual drug store lease calls for a percentage of sales or a guaranteed minimum, whichever is greater. Usually for the departmentalized type of drug store, this percentage is 3 percent. For the pharmacy type of operation, the percentage may range from 5 to 8 percent. The guaranteed minimum rental will range from $1.50

to $2.50 per square foot per year, depending on the size and location of the store.

Recently, in getting leases for a shopping center, we needed a drug store. There were several listed in our book of chain stores that might conceivably be interested in the area, and we wrote all of them a preliminary letter. One of these chains answered that they were very interested in expanding in that area. We accordingly sent them a map showing the location of the shopping center and a proposed plan for its development. As a result of this, their real estate representative came to visit us, looked over the location and approved it. He asked us to make a lease proposal to his company, which we did. After negotiation, a lease was agreed upon which called for a 7,500 square foot drug store at a rental of $15,000 per year or 3½ percent of sales, whichever is larger. Since the lease is fifteen years, the owner can borrow the total cost of construction and more on the lease and make a very sizable return on his investment.

Shoe Stores

There are a great number of chain stores in the country that are vigorously expanding their number of shoe stores. There are several types of shoe stores, but the most numerous is the family type of store which carries shoes for every member of the family. These stores usually require a floor space of from two to four or five thousand square feet depending on the amount of business that the chain thinks it can obtain in any particular location. These leases are usually for ten to fifteen years and carry a percentage of sales, usually 5 percent, as against a minimum guaranteed rental. These stores are interested in downtown locations and shopping center locations, but very seldom are interested in free standing stores in neighborhood areas.

In finding leases for a shopping center, we needed a shoe store, so several shoe chains were contacted by letter. Several expressed interest, and we followed this up with a second letter showing maps and diagrams and asking them for certain information about their stores. After reviewing the information sent us by these companies, we decided that the one that had a family type of shoe store was best suited for our center, and we made them a lease proposal. The shoe chain wanted an exclusive in the shopping center which we were not willing to give entirely. After negotiation, the lease wound up with a store of 3,000 square feet at a rental of $9,000 per year or 5 percent of sales, whichever was greater, with the chain to have the only shoe store in the center until the total size of the center reached 125,000 square feet of retail area, after which time we could have a second shoe store if the owner considered it desirable.

Variety Stores

The comparatively small five and ten cent store is growing more and more scarce. The big companies that used to have this type of store, such as Woolworth, Kresge, W. T. Grant Co., etc. are now going to larger stores which are more in the nature of department stores than the old five and ten. There are, however, a few chains left that do put up these comparatively small type of variety stores. Probably the majority of them are franchise stores and are owned by the operator of the store; however, in most cases the parent company will cosign the lease.

The stores are interested in from four to eight thousand square feet in the neighborhoods where there are many homes. They especially like neighborhoods where they do not have competition from the larger stores.

Clothing Stores

There are a very great number of chain stores in the clothing business. These are stores of all types. Some of them handle only men's clothing, some of them only women's clothing and some of them handle both. There are also chains of stores that handle nothing but clothes for children. Some specialize in sports clothes, some specialize in clothes for teen-agers, etc.

The size of these stores will range from about two thousand square feet up to maybe twenty or twenty-five thousand, depending on the area where the store is and on the policy of that particular company.

It is comparatively rare for any of these to be franchise operations. These types of stores are interested in downtown locations or shopping centers, but are seldom interested in neighborhood shopping areas.

Recently in an excellent shopping area, we noticed that one firm had three stores, one of these stores handling men's clothing, one women's clothing and one children's clothing. It seemed much better if they would consolidate into one operation, and we were able to find where they could obtain a much larger building and put all three of the leases in one. After considerable negotiation, this was effected on a basis of a 26,000 square foot store on a fifteen year lease with a minimum guaranteed rental of $39,000 per year or a rental of 3 percent of gross sales, whichever was larger. The operation of the clothing company was vastly improved by this, as they were able to lower their total payroll and other costs of doing business due to the fact that their operations were all under one roof. The return to the owner of the property was increased, since the cost of a large building is less per square foot than on smaller buildings.

Department Stores

There are a number of large chains that are expanding rapidly in the department store field. These stores range in size from fifty thousand square feet to two hundred thousand. Some of the big chains are going into the very large stores. These department stores carry everything conceivable. They will have restaurants, automobile service stores, all types of clothing, furniture, household goods, sporting goods and even in some cases a complete line of groceries.

While these stores are practically all company operated stores, some of the stores do have departments which are leased out. Frequently this is the case with the shoe department or the millinery or other specialized departments.

These companies require a parking ratio of at least three or four square feet of parking area for every square foot of their building area. For this reason, a store of one hundred thousand square feet requires an overall area of four hundred thousand square feet or nearly ten acres. These stores quite frequently will have free standing locations in well-populated areas where streets leading to the store are adequate to carry heavy traffic and where the access is convenient. It is not necessary for these stores to have any other businesses in the immediate vicinity.

There are also some who like to expand in shopping center locations that have as many other businesses in the same location as possible.

The usual lease for these stores is at least fifteen to twenty years and is a percentage of sales or a minimum guarantee, whichever is larger. The usual percentage can vary from 2 to 3 percent and the amount of money paid per square foot presently will run from $1.25 to $1.75. These stores are not expensive to build per square foot and therefore do not command as high a rent as smaller and more expensive stores.

The expansion used to be only in towns of one hundred thousand people or more. However in recent years these types of operations have been expanding to towns even as small as fifteen thousand people. The location, however, must be a good one so that the drawing territory for the store can be large enough to support it.

There are a great many large, well-financed discount chains that are expanding their operations substantially. We found a location of about ten acres, properly zoned for business, which seemed to us a good one for a discount operation. Accordingly, we took our chain store book and wrote to real estate managers of about ten or twelve of these department store chains that we thought might be interested in our area. Nearly all of these chains answered us, and three or four expressed interest. Here again, we followed this up with a map of the city and some economic information about the area and then followed these letters up with telephone calls. As a result, representatives of three different companies came to see us and viewed the location. After considerable negotiations, we made a lease with one of these firms for a 75,000 square foot store for fifteen years at a rental of 2½ percent of gross sales or $100,000 per year rental, whichever was larger. The owner of the land built a building to suit the specifications of the department store chain. These buildings are comparatively economical to build, since they are one large room without expensive construction features. Such a deal is profitable to everyone concerned.

Miscellaneous Stores

There are a number of other different types of stores such as fabric shops, sewing machine centers, trading stamp redemption stores, and many others. Most of these stores like to be in neighborhoods where there are other businesses nearby, so that they can draw from as much traffic in the immediate location as possible.

POINTS TO KEEP IN MIND

It is necessary, in order to obtain leases, to be familiar with the various chain stores that are in the area where the property is located and to know what type of properties each of these chains needs. The most rapidly expanding types of chain stores are:

- Restaurants
- Dry Cleaners
- Banks
- Drug Stores
- Shoe Stores
- Variety Stores
- Clothing Stores
- Department Stores

Chapter 9

Leasing Franchise Stores: An Amazing Profit-Multiplier

One of the fastest growing types of store is the franchise operation. The advantage of the franchise is that it gives a retail concern a chance to expand very rapidly with a minimum of capital required. The franchise holder puts up most or all of the capital. The advantage to the franchise holder is that he can open a business of his own with direction and counsel from a successful large concern in that line of business.

Due to the rapid spread of franchise operations, it is an unusually good field for anyone obtaining leases. Franchise operations are good for highway locations, shopping center locations, neighborhood locations, or in some cases, free standing stores.

Neighborhood Groceries

There has been a vast growth in the small grocery store. These stores are primarily for convenient shopping. Where the housewife only wants to buy two or three items, it is very inconvenient to go through a large supermarket, and she would much prefer to deal with a small neighborhood store. These stores remain open longer hours, usually seven days a week.

These small stores like to be in residential neighborhoods and do not necessarily have to have any other businesses in the immediate location, as long as the store is convenient to many residents and has sufficient parking. These stores are usually about three to four thousand square feet in size with parking for anywhere from ten to twenty-five cars.

Most of these are franchise operations, although there are some which are company operated. There are several of these chains, none of them national, but some are very strong regional and local outfits.

Recently I noticed that a chain operator of neighborhood groceries had opened a unit in my area. This type of operator normally likes to have several units in the same area so that their advertising cost can be spread over several stores. We immediately started looking for other locations for this group, and we were able to find one in a neighborhood shopping center that did not have a store of this type. It is located in a residential area with 800 to 1,000 homes that are directly served by that location.

We found out from the manager of the unit that was already opened who was the real estate manager of the concern and contacted him by phone. We thought our location would be of immediate interest, it was and a lease was made, completed and signed by everybody in less than a week. The terms of it were for a store of 3,200 square feet with a rental of $6,400 per year or 3 percent of sales, whichever was higher. Since the store required no unusual features, it did not cost much to finish, and the result is an excellent return for the owner of the property.

Variety Stores

A great many of the small ten cent stores that you see around the country are owned by the person who operates the store and who is operating under the name of a larger company on a franchise arrangement. Usually this arrangement calls for giving the owner of the store the right to use the company's name, and the main company guarantees the lease. For these services, the owner of the store is compelled to buy all of his merchandise from the parent company who, in effect, operates as wholesale distributors. They are interested in neighborhood shopping areas where they can be the only store of the type in the immediate area.

Restaurants

A large percentage of the restaurant chains expand through the franchise store procedure. One reason for this is the large amount of capital involved in opening some of the new restaurant units. It is estimated that the total cost of land, building and equipment for a good drive-in restaurant will run in the neighborhood of $150,000. By acquiring franchise holders who have capital, the chain is relieved from the necessity of raising a large amount of capital for each unit opened.

Frequently these stores are operated on a three-way deal, with a group of investors buying land, constructing the building and leasing it to the operator, who in turn, operates under a franchise from the parent company.

Recently, we made a three-way lease deal that was very profitable for everyone. The owner of some land on an access road from an interstate and near a good residential area wanted an income from it. We were able to make a fifty-year lease on this land with some people who wanted to build and in turn lease to a drive-in restaurant. The owner of the land leased it to some builders who constructed the building, who in turn leased the building to an individual who wanted to start a restaurant, and the individual in turn took a franchise from a nationally known concern. The lease terms in this case amounted to $2.25 per square foot of restaurant area or 5 percent of sales, whichever was greater.

Auto Supply Stores

Probably the majority of the auto supply stores in the country are franchise operations. This, of course, is not true of the auto supply departments in the big department stores that frequently have a T.B.A. store (tires, batteries and accessories), which is a separate automobile store with a service department.

However, some of the largest chains have associate stores, and most of the auto supply stores that you see are of this kind. These stores prefer a downtown location or one in a shopping center. They require service bays, sometimes on the side or in the rear, so that the tires and accessories can be installed on the customers' cars. For this reason, it is sometimes difficult to find a location that suits this type of business.

Hardware Stores

Several of the large wholesale hardware concerns are expanding into the retail business by means of franchise operations. Usually the procedure here is the same as with auto supply stores or variety stores. The parent company helps find the location for the store, helps supervise its opening and requires the franchise holder to purchase their merchandise from the parent company. In return for this, the parent company's name can be used and usually the parent company will have experts to help in the advertising of the franchise operation and in the training of its personnel, etc. These concerns are interested in shopping centers, neighborhood stores, or especially in small towns, in downtown stores.

Recently, we had a location in a part of town that we thought would be ideal for a hardware business. In line with the usual practice of doing this, we contacted several chains by letter. Those who expressed interest received a second letter with maps showing the location, and this second letter was followed up by a telephone call. One of our telephone calls immediately bore fruit, and the real estate manager of the chain came to see us. He was interested in the location provided he could find a franchise holder who would actually operate the store.

It so happened that we were in touch with a gentleman with sufficient capital who was interested in getting into the hardware business, and we managed to get the individual and the franchise company together with the result that a lease was made. An old building was used that required some remodeling, although not a great deal, and the rental terms of $1.50 per square foot per year or 3 percent of sales, whichever was greater, was a very profitable one to the landowner.

HOW TO CONTACT CHAINS

Form Letters

You should have a copy of the latest directory of leading chain stores published by the Chain Store Business Guide. These books are available through the National Association of Realtors and list most of the chain stores found in the United States. They can be purchased by anyone. These stores are listed by states and by cities where their headquarters are located. Information includes the number of stores, the officers of the company, and in which states they are operating.

By going through this book and picking the type of companies which you think would be interested in your area and picking out those that seem to be expanding in that vicinity, you can get an effective mailing list. Direct your form letter to the officer that you think would be the one responsible for finding real estate locations. Sometimes there is an officer mentioned in this guide who is the real estate specialist and, of course, the letter would be addressed to him; otherwise, it probably is best to write to whoever is president of the corporation.

The information that should be covered in your letter must include the location that you have in mind and some information about the trade area. Usually a brochure from your local Chamber of Commerce is all the information that is necessary, since these chains will have their own sources of market information. You also should indicate to them the parking that will be available and whether or not the store can be designed to any specifications they wish. It is helpful to give them an idea of the date the premises will be available.

A sample of a letter actually used to mail to chains is Exhibit 9-1.

Mr. John Smith, Real Estate Manager
Jones & Jones Corporation
200 Brown Avenue
New York, New York

Dear Mr. Smith:

Thomasville is now the fourth largest market in our state. It has a total immediate marketing area of over one hundred thousand people with a wider territory of tributary cities from which to draw.

Business is thriving in Thomasville and is supported by income from agriculture, industry, and commerce. I feel that this market needs one of your stores and that it would be a highly profitable location for you.

The location I have in mind is ideal for your type of business, and the owner will build to suit your specifications. You would be guaranteed a three-to-one parking ratio, and I am sure we could arrange lease terms that would be suitable for you.

If you would like a map of our city showing the exact location and a plat of the immediate area, let me know and I will send it to you.

Very truly yours,

Sample Letter to Chain Store
Exhibit 9-1

Phone Calls

These form letters can be followed up by telephone calls where you think advisable. Generally speaking, the real estate offices of these corporations are extremely busy and are constantly bombarded by letters and phone calls from different people. For this reason, it is sometimes rather difficult to get their attention. Phone calls should definitely be made to them when you receive an answer to your form letter. Usually it is best to answer this letter by a letter and a phone call both, so as to make a deeper impression on the person you are contacting.

An idea of how a telephone conversation might go is something like his:

"Hello, Mr. Jones. You undoubtedly received my letter regarding the very fine location in Smithville. Did I send you enough information for you to decide to what extent you have an interest?"

Mr. Jones may reply, "I received your letter, but did not get enough information as to the exact location and very little information about rental terms."

"I can send you a map and a plat of the area and will get it in the mail today. On rental terms, much would depend on the size of building and what your specifications require. What size store would you have in mind?"

"Most of our stores have about 25,000 square feet and do not require any extra construction costs."

"In that case, Mr. Jones, I think I can arrange a store for somewhere in the vicinity of $1.50 per square foot per year against the usual percentage, but I would have to see your specifications to be sure. Do you think you can plan a trip to see us and look at the location in person? I am sure if you can do this, you would like it."

"I will try to get away next week to come and see you."

"Be sure and let me know as far as possible in advance."

"I will let you know just as soon as I know myself when I can get away."

"Looking forward to seeing you."

Local Managers

If any of the chains in which you are interested have local branches, usually you can get information as to their plans for expansion from the manager of their local store. It is a good idea for you to get acquainted with him, and frequently he can tell you the individual that is most advantageous for you to contact and in what areas the chain is most interested. In this way you can attract the attention of the proper person.

Neighboring Towns

Frequently you can get leads as to which chains are interested in expanding in your community by knowing what they are doing in neighboring towns in the same general trade area. If the city in which you are located is a small one, frequently you can get leads from your nearest larger city. Sometimes these chains will have a store in a large city that they have had for several years, and they are interested in expanding to smaller towns in the same state or in the same general geographical area.

Chamber of Commerce and Trade Associations

Frequently chains who are interested in expanding in your area will write to the Chamber of Commerce in your city for information. Sometimes they will also request that they be put in contact with a reputable real estate broker.

If you are a broker and also a member of your local Chamber of Commerce, you can get a number of leads in this way. If there are any trade associations, with offices in your city, it is a good idea to be acquainted with the manager of these associations, since you can frequently get leads that way also.

POINTS TO KEEP IN MIND

Franchise stores are stores owned by individuals for which they have a franchise with a larger concern.

- Leading types of franchise stores are:
  - Neighborhood Groceries
  - Variety Stores
  - Restaurants
  - Auto Supply Stores
  - Hardware Stores
- Chain stores can be contacted by mail, by telephone calls or by personal calls.

Chapter 10

The Wonderful Potential in Service Station Leasing

GROWTH

The immense increase in the number of service stations along the nation's highways and streets in recent years is obvious to anyone. The competition between oil companies for good service station locations has been such that in some spots you will find as many as five or six stations in a single block. Since most of these station locations are occupied by large oil companies with immense financial resources, oil company leases are very lucrative and represent a large profit potential to the property owner or to the agent who arranges the deal. There are several reasons why this growth in the number of stations has been so phenomenal.

Increased Prosperity

With more people in the nation and with increased incomes, the number of automobiles on our streets and highways has shown a large increase. Along with this increased prosperity, the movement of merchandise has resulted in an increase in the number of trucks.

Also in recent years there has been the tendency toward shorter work weeks with resulting additional leisure time and this, coupled with additional income, has resulted in an increase in mileage for the average car. The tendency toward longer vacations has led to increased interstate travel. The growth in resort areas, the increase in the number of vacation homes, the traffic to and from lakes and rivers due to the popularity of boating are just a few of the factors that have increased highway traffic. There has also been a sizable increase in horsepower per car, which leads to more gas consumption. The increased number of air-conditioned cars has also led to increased gasoline consumption. In order to supply this insatiable demand for gasoline, it has been necessary to have many more service stations.

Road Changes and Traffic Patterns

The big development from the point of view of oil companies has been the growth of the interstate system. This network of express highways, which will eventually connect all of the major cities of the nation, has itself contributed to a growth in the number of miles traveled by automobiles and has thus helped to increase gasoline consumption. It has also had the effect of drawing much traffic away from older highways. This has meant that more companies have found it necessary to relocate their service stations in order to serve the huge amount of traffic on these interstates. Since access is controlled on the interstates, the only convenient place for service stations is at exists and entrances, so that the traveler can pull off the interstate, obtain his gasoline and then pull back on. At some of these interchanges, you will see as many as five or six or more different companies with service stations. This change in traffic patterns on our highways has resulted in the closing of many stations on the older roads and the building of thousands of new ones on the interstates.

Another change in highway patterns that has been very important has been the continued and increasing move to the suburbs. Since convenient mass transportation is usually lacking, most of the people living in the suburbs drive back and forth to work or back and forth to downtown in private automobiles. In order to move this large amount of traffic to and from various areas within the cities each day, it has been necessary to build many expressways, circles and bypasses, etc. All of this has caused the oil companies to build many thousands of new stations to serve the traffic on these new routes.

WHAT OIL COMPANIES WANT

In order to take the most advantage of the opportunities for possible leasing to oil companies, it is necessary to know what these companies want. They all have definite yardsticks and sets of specifications that they use in finding locations. There are a number of things that are important in determining where they will put a service station and where they will not put one.

Traffic

Obviously it is important to oil companies to have their service stations where there is a lot of vehicle traffic. The emphasis now is on the interstate system, since it is recognized that most through travel in the United States will go by these primary superhighways. Some of these highways carry more traffic than others and, of course, those with the most traffic will also have the most service stations. The preferred locations are at interchanges, and the preferred interchange locations are the ones closest to the interstates. The access roads leading from the superhighway have controlled access and are fenced for a certain distance from the interstate highway itself. The very first lots at the end of this controlled access are the most desirable ones. There are four of these lots, and it is not unusual to see service stations on every one of them as well as on the lots adjoining.

These interchanges are also good locations for restaurants and motels, and frequently there will be a cooperative deal worked out whereby there would be a motel and a restaurant and a service station all adjoining. A number of the oil companies have made arrangements to cooperate with certain motel chains in the matter of finding locations. Also many of the oil companies have restaurant divisions, so that when they find a location at an interstate interchange, they get one big enough to have not only a service station, but also a restaurant.

In hunting for locations that can be sold to oil companies, corner lots on any of the interstate interchanges will usually be desirable. In the event the four corners have already been taken by oil companies, acquire the ones next to the corners. Once you get an option or a listing on a lot at an interchange, you can then take it up with the companies that are not already represented at that particular interchange. Any of the major companies that operate in the area of the interchange are good prospects. We were able to locate a lot at a very busy interchange where there were already five service stations. By process of elimination, it was very simple to tell which company would be most interested in the lots still available. The lot was presented to this company and the deal was made very quickly.

Other locations that oil companies like are on good streets or highways leading from substantial residential developments to the downtown areas. The best way to find a location on these arteries that would be salable to oil companies is to find out what lots are zoned and bring it to the attention of those that are not yet represented on this particular street.

Neighborhood Business

Frequently oil companies will take locations that are not on busy traffic streets, but that are easily accessible from large residential areas. What they are catering to in these locations is the local neighborhood business and not the through traffic. The best way to determine lots that are available for this is through your zoning map which will show you what areas are zoned. Usually if there is a good service station already in a neighborhood location, it is difficult to sell another one unless the first one is doing an unusually fine business, in which case another oil company may think it can get enough business there also.

Size of Lots

Generally speaking, oil company locations are getting larger all the time. About the smallest lot which an oil company is interested in now would be one 150 feet square if it is on a corner. If the lot is not on a corner, they would want a larger frontage. Usually the oil company will have several pumps and two or three bays for lubrication and other car services. They also would like to have at least two entrances, and very wide entrances at that. This is the reason why they require large lots.

Other Considerations Pertaining to Location

The matter of proper zoning is essential, and this is becoming more important in urban areas. In order to control growth in an orderly manner, the zoning boards in most cities are becoming more strict in that it has become more difficult to get a zoning changed once it has been set. Very few oil companies will take an option on a piece of property that is not zoned, unless they have some very good reason for thinking they can get the zoning changed.

Another requirement for most oil stations is that it be on a city sewer. This is not necessarily a requirement of the oil company, but will be a requirement of the building inspector of the city.

HOW TO FIND LOCATIONS FOR OIL COMPANIES AND HOW TO PRESENT THESE LOCATIONS TO THEM

One of the most useful tools you can have in trying to locate suitable sites is a zoning map. By the use of the zoning map, you can pick out places where it is possible to have service stations, and then visit those areas. If there is some vacant property in business zoning in a traffic area, then you can probably go to the city engineer's office and get a traffic count of that street. If it looks as though there is enough business in that area to support one or more gas stations, it might be worthwhile to carry the matter further.

Competition

The first step would be to check the competition from service stations already in business in that area. If there are other service stations, are these stations busy and prosperous or do they look deserted. If the traffic is heavy enough and if the stations there all seem to be very busy and prosperous, there might be room for another one. If, however, you see a station that is vacant with a "For Rent" sign on it, it is probably best to forget that area and try to get a better one.

Contacting Owners

If, by this time, you feel that there is a logical reason for another service station in that area, then the next step would be to contact the owners of the vacant properties which have the proper zoning. Some of the properties can be immediately eliminated as they will be too small for service station use or, in some cases, too large but not large enough to subdivide. You can then talk to the owners to see if you find any of them that are interested in doing something with their vacant property.

Most oil companies now prefer to buy the real estate, and if one of the owners is interested in selling and has property the right size and has priced it within reason, this is probably your best bet. If, however, the owner of the best location prefers to lease his land, many oil companies will lease the ground on a long-term lease and build their own station on it. There will also be certain owners who will prefer to build the station for the oil company on a long-term lease. Many oil companies are interested in doing this also.

In any event, be sure to find out first what the owner wants to do; then you can determine your own course of action. If the owner wants to sell and puts an attractive price on his property, it would pay you to get an option on it long enough to see whether or not it can be sold to an oil company at profit. If he prefers to lease to the oil company or build and lease to them, you can operate on a fee or commission basis.

The owner will undoubtedly have a plat of his property, and it is essential that you have one of these in order to present the matter properly to the oil companies. While you are getting the option on the individual's property or getting a commission agreement, you should also get a copy of this plat as you will definitely need it later.

Who to Contact in the Oil Company

By making a survey of the area and seeing what stations are there, you can usually determine which oil companies are not well represented in that area and who would therefore be your best prospects. It is helpful to pinpoint on a map the location of competing stations and make a list of the companies that own them. The ones that are conspicuous by their absence would then be logical prospects.

While all of the major oil companies have separate real estate departments and their own employees who specialize in finding locations, they also have district managers that have a great deal to say about how and where their company expands in that district. It is usually best to contact the district manager first by a personal call. Show him a map of the city and exactly where the site is located, give him a traffic count or any other information that seems of value and show him the plat of the property. While the district manager will not have the final say as to whether or not the oil company makes a deal on the location you have in mind, his opinion on it will carry a great deal of weight. After you have sold the district manager on the location, go directly to the real estate man in charge of that area. Usually this man will work out of a district or regional office and may be located a considerable distance from you. If, however, he is located close to you, a personal call will certainly be worthwhile. If you must send him information about the location by mail, be sure to send a map of the city showing the exact location, a plat of the property involved and a letter telling him that the property is zoned properly. Remember to mention that it has city sewers and that his district manager thinks it is an excellent location.

Since these real estate managers get dozens of letters every day from people presenting locations to them, it is difficult to get their undivided attention on one piece of property. For that reason, you should call them by phone not later than the day after they get your information. By reminding them over the phone about it, you can get them to pay more attention to what you have sent them. When talking to the real estate manager, find out when he is going to be in your area so that you can meet with him and personally show him this property and the advantages that it holds as a location for one of his stations.

OIL COMPANY OPTION PROCEDURES

All major oil companies have standardized procedures that they use in purchasing or leasing property. The essential feature of these procedures is an option. The oil company, if it is interested in the property, will take first an option usually for a minimum period of ninety days which gives it the right to purchase or lease the property at any time during that period. During the term of the option, the oil company makes exhaustive surveys and studies of the location to determine for sure that it is the one that they want. Then the real estate manager with whom you are dealing sends all of the information about the property that he has, including the survey that his company has made, to the next higher office, which is usually a regional office. This regional office studies the material submitted by their district office and either decides immediately to reject the property or to buy it, or they may decide that some of the executives from the regional office should come and look at the property before making a decision. After the regional office passes on the property, the proposition is sent to the main office of the company for final approval or rejection. Actually the important office to decide on the matter is the regional office, as 98 percent of the time the head office of the company will follow the recommendations of the regional office. So far in my experience, there has never been an instance when the main office has reversed a regional office decision.

Due to the complicated procedure of getting a final decision on a piece of property, the option is considered absolutely necessary by oil companies. They invest a considerable amount of money in making surveys of the location and having their various employees travel to look at it; and without having the property tied up with an option, they can frequently go to all this trouble and expense, decide to buy the property, and then find that it has already been sold to someone else.

Option Terms

Most oil companies will insist on a minimum principle term of the option of ninety days, and they will probably have a clause in the option giving them an automatic extension of time, should it be necessary. There must be, of course, a consideration for the option and whatever money is paid for this consideration applies on the purchase price should the property be purchased, or if the option is not exercised, this amount is forfeited. All oil companies try to get these option payments as low as possible and do get a great many options for the nominal sum of $1.00, $5.00 or $10.00. However, if the property is desirable and the oil company likes it, they will make an option consideration of a substantial amount up to several hundred dollars. Many of the oil companies will insist that they do not make payments for options, but most of them do and if you insist on it and they like the property, you can get option considerations of several hundred dollars. It is a good idea to get as large an option payment as possible because the larger the investment of the oil company in the option payment, the more attention they will pay to that particular property. In this case they will make their surveys very promptly and reach a decision sooner. No employee of an oil company likes to see an option payment forfeited, as he thinks this might be considered a black eye to him, so he will work much harder to try to get a piece of property approved by his company if there is a large option payment involved.

There will always be a clause in the option about title to the property. Some oil companies make the owners furnish them with title insurance and others have their own legal department look up and certify the title.

There is always a clause relating to how the deal is to be closed in the event the oil company exercises its option. In the event that it is a lease that is under consideration, the terms of the lease will be set forth very carefully. If it is the purchase of the property, usually the clause will set forth that the purchase price is to be paid in cash, to whom paid and that the deed is to be passed at the same time.

Usually an oil company option is a rather formidable looking document with fine print and many different provisions. The oil companies are usually elastic about these provisions and if there is anything that the owner objects to and seems unfair to him, you can usually get the oil company to change the provision.

How to Get a Property Owner to Sign the Option

The first step in presenting an option to an owner is to explain to him the reasons why it is essential for the oil company to have it. You can also explain to him the advantages of selling to an oil company. These advantages are that the company will pay cash, or in the event of a lease, will make their rental payments promptly and they will, in almost all instances, pay top price for the property. Actually the increase in property values in many places has been caused by oil companies bidding against each other and thereby forcing property values up. It should be easy to convince the owner that he is going to get a better deal from oil companies than from anyone else.

In the event that you have been able to get the oil company to put up a sizable deposit on the option, this is a great inducement in getting the owner to sign since he knows that he is going to make at least something out of the deal no matter what happens. Some owners, while they understand the reason for the oil company needing the option, are reluctant to sign it due to the fact that it is a lengthy document. Many people have a fear of signing a document because they are afraid they might be tricked. These people either do not trust their own judgment in reading an option or, as is the case many times, the owner is confused by the legal phraseology used.

If you will go over the option, paragraph by paragraph, and explain it to the owner, sometimes this will solve the problem. As a last resort, if you can't get him to sign it otherwise, you can take the option to his attorney and have the attorney give him his opinion on it.

When you talk to the owner about signing the option, it should be completely filled in and ready for signature and, in the last analysis, the main reason why he should sign it is that he has an excellent chance of accomplishing what he wants with his land. You can explain to him that oil companies seldom take options unless they actually want to complete a deal on the property. The oil companies do not want to waste their time and money any more than anyone else does, and most of them seldom take options without a sincere belief that the option will be exercised. In my experience, about 85 percent of the options taken by oil companies are exercised.

One of the frequent objections that owners have to these options is the automatic renewal clause. Recently we had a case like this in which everything was apparently agreed upon, but the owner objected strenuously to the fact that the oil company, in addition to their ninety days, had an automatic thirty-day extension clause. We suggested to the oil company that they make an additional option payment in case they needed this extra thirty days. This was agreeable to them, and we explained to the owner that he could have an extra amount of money paid by the oil company if they exercised this option. He was perfectly agreeable, the option was signed and soon resulted in a completed deal.

Closing the Transaction

Closing transactions of this kind are very simple. The oil company will have its own attorney who has already satisfied himself with the title or title insurance, as the case may be. The oil company has completed its surveys and has all of the information it needs about the property. Recently we closed a deal of this kind in less than three minutes. All it amounted to was that the owner handed the deed to the oil company attorney, who had already examined the deed; the oil company attorney handed the owner a check, and that ended the matter.

POINTS TO KEEP IN MIND

- There is a great opportunity for investors and for real estate agents in selling or leasing property to oil companies, due to the great expansion of service stations.
- The oil companies want locations properly zoned where there is heavy traffic or much neighborhood business.

- Finding locations is comparatively easy by means of a zoning map and visits to the various properly zoned locations.
- In presenting locations to oil companies, take up the matter of the location with the manager of your local district and with the real estate manager of the oil company.
- In getting an option signed, know the provisions of the option and be able to explain it to the property owner.

Chapter 11

Guaranteed Profits from Main Street Leases

Until the development of the shopping center, leases in the downtown commercial areas of cities were the only ones of sufficient amounts and with terms long enough to be highly important to the investor or the agent. Today, in spite of the huge development in shopping centers, downtown leases can still be worthwhile.

FUTURE OF DOWNTOWN SHOPPING AREAS

Due to the growth of suburbs spreading farther away from downtown areas and the increase in suburban shopping centers, there has been a great deal of concern as to the future of the downtown area. Not only have more people been moving away from the center of the city, but the ones moving are, generally speaking, in the higher income group. All retail businesses have been effected. However, there will undoubtedly be a downtown shopping area for a good many reasons.

Advantages of Downtown Locations

There are certain types of businesses that remain in the downtown area and probably will continue to stay there. These will always draw a number of people. There are many types of offices, such as government offices, lawyers' offices, stock exchange offices and others that tend to remain in the downtown area. The biggest department stores, the biggest hotels and the largest theatres also tend to remain in the congested downtown area. The presence of these strong drawing cards also creates an opportunity for smaller shops of all kinds. These smaller shops, such as gift shops, jewelry stores, specialty clothing stores and many other kinds, locate where their window display space can be seen by the people who are attracted to the downtown area by the big traffic pullers.

Another advantage of the downtown area is that it is usually centrally located and is the central point for mass transportation service. Subway or surface car or bus lines radiate from the downtown area to all parts of the city, and it is usually easier to get to the downtown area from any particular suburb than to get to another suburb in the same metropolitan area.

Disadvantages of Downtown Areas

Disadvantages of downtown areas are fairly obvious. The principal one is, of course, lack of parking. In many cities this is remedied to a large extent by tearing down old buildings and building parking lots or multi-story parking garages. This development is very helpful to the downtown area and will preserve it as a good shopping district for an indefinite time in the future.

Another disadvantage of downtown is the fact that so many buildings are very old and unattractive. There have not been very many new buildings erected in the downtown areas of most cities. This is not true of all of them, as many cities such as Atlanta, Georgia, for instance, have a great many new and attractive buildings. The old building disadvantage is one that can be overcome. Frequently, long-term leases have been made in downtown areas in the past and these leases are still in effect. Due to the gradual inflation that has taken place in the past several years, the fixed dollar rentals on leases made many years ago are of very little value today. In fact there are instances of old and long-term leases in downtown areas where the rent no longer pays the taxes. Under these conditions, the landlord does not feel very anxious about modernizing his property and tends to make as few improvements as possible.

Another disadvantage of downtown areas is so frequently the lack of public transportation. When each person drives to the downtown area in a car, the main streets leading to and from are often quite congested and travel is made very difficult. Even though there has been parking provided in the downtown area, it is still difficult to get there and back.

CLASSIFICATION OF MAIN STREET LOCATIONS

In small size cities, the downtown shopping area is confined to a few blocks and is actually not divided into different areas. However in larger cities, the downtown area is usually divided into a theatre and hotel district and a shopping district.

Theatre and Hotel District

In most large cities, the downtown theatres tend to be in the same general area. Also in this area are to be found many restaurants and night clubs. It might be classified as the entertainment part of the city.

There could be quite a number of small retail stores also in this area, usually a drug store, gift shops, novelty shops, jewelry stores, and specialty clothing stores. It is where the facilities for evening entertainment can be found.

Rents in this district are quite high, but there is heavy traffic, especially in the evening, which justifies these high rates.

Downtown hotels also tend to group in a relatively small area. In this area you find restaurants and a number of retail stores of all kinds. Usually, however, it is not the main shopping district.

Shopping District

This is the area of the city where one finds the big department stores, sometimes occupying as much as two city blocks with one store. Preferred locations for all types of other businesses are in this general shopping area. Clothing stores, shoe stores, jewelry stores, book stores, and almost every conceivable kind of retail business will be located in this area. In recent years there has been a great attempt to increase the parking facilities in the shopping area by means of parking lots or multi-story garages. However, the area still is usually very congested and difficult to reach. It is the area of the city with heaviest pedestrian traffic.

PHYSICAL ASPECTS OF DOWNTOWN LOCATIONS

An overall characteristic of downtown business property is the fact that there is very little vacant land, and most good locations already have buildings on it. Unless the owner will consider tearing down an old building and constructing a new one in its place, the question becomes one of whether or not the present building is suitable or can be remodeled to suit the particular use for it.

Size

No two businesses need exactly the same size rooms, so the matter of size of any downtown building is very important. There has been a tendency in recent years toward larger and larger stores, and sometimes it works out very well if you can get two or three downtown buildings which adjoin and which can be, with sufficient remodeling, thrown into one larger building. Naturally the matter of the number of stories and height enters importantly into the matter. If the building is narrow, usually the upper floors are of very little value except for storage. In a large building suitable for a department store, eight or ten floors can be used if there are enough elevators and escalators.

In certain downtown areas, store buildings do not have entrances from the rear. This is a very considerable objection because receiving merchandise in the front door interferes with the normal movement of trade. The larger the store, the more essential the rear entrance becomes. If there is an alley behind the store, is it wide enough to accommodate large trucks? If you are considering making a large building from two or three smaller ones, the project probably would not be feasible unless there is a rear entrance.

Remodeling

Most of the downtown stores are old and in many cases have completely outdated fronts and show windows. An important point to consider is how much the cost would be to put in a modern front with modern show windows. Other improvements that should be made include air-conditioning, and the cost of it should be carefully checked. Usually a downtown building with modern facilities and a modern front will bring about twice the rent of an older building which does not have the up-to-date equipment. If it is a multi-story building, escalators and elevators become essential, and the condition and number of them is important. If the number of them is insufficient, what would be the cost of installing some more equipment?

WHO WANTS DOWNTOWN LOCATIONS

A large downtown area will usually contain various kinds of retail stores. However, the ones that actually prefer downtown and will usually locate there rather than in the suburban shopping centers are:

1. Department Stores
2. Book Stores
3. Specialty Clothing Stores
4. Jewelry Stores
5. Cafeterias
6. Candy Stores
7. Engravers
8. Office Equipment
9. Optical Stores
10. Office Furniture and Equipment
11. Other stores that sell shopper's type items

Your best prospects for possible leases in a downtown area will come from the groups mentioned here.

HOW TO LOCATE TENANTS FOR DOWNTOWN PROPERTIES

At one time, the demand for store space in downtown areas was very large and filled every available square foot. However, such is not the case today, and in almost all downtown areas you will notice a number of vacant buildings. If you can find a good tenant for any of these vacant buildings, it is probably a good purchase or a good project for an agent.

Stores Already in the Downtown Area

The most obvious source of prospects for downtown leases, although it is a source that is frequently overlooked, is the store that is already there. Frequently an existing store needs more space or a better location or the building in which it is located is not modern enough.

Frequently a successful store, located in an old and out-of-date building, would like to move. Some landlords do not want to spend money in upgrading their property, with the result that their store remains with an out-of-date front and a decaying unpleasant appearance. A great deal of downtown property in most cities is also owned by estates in the hands of trustees who either do not have the power to remodel or who do not want to do so.

By getting an old, run-down vacant building and remodeling it and putting in a modern front, you can frequently get a good deal from a tenant who is already in the downtown area, but in an old and dilapidated structure.

Another source of leases would be where there is a vacant store adjoining one occupied by a prosperous tenant. If this tenant should need extra space in which to expand, it might be feasible to combine the two storerooms and give the existing tenant an extra area. Problems present themselves in this sort of thing, but they can be worked out.

Branches of Out of Town Stores

A survey of downtown areas in other nearby cities or a study of the phone book of these cities will reveal certain firms that are not represented locally. By noticing the size of the various firms that are in neighboring cities but not in your locality, you can soon narrow the list down to the ones that would be interested in the size of building which is available in your downtown area. The most numerous prospects for this type of expansion are chain store companies that like to be represented in all possible markets. However, frequently there are local merchants in the neighboring cities who have progressed as far as they can in their one store and would like to have another one not too far away.

DOWNTOWN LEASES

While downtown space is not in the demand that it was in the past, property values in many cities are often lower, with the result that a downtown lease still is profitable to the owner or agent.

Terms

One change in recent years concerning downtown leases has been a shortening of the period covered by the lease. Formerly, the tenant was anxious to get as long a lease as possible due to the demands for downtown property and feeling that it would always be good as the community grew. This is no longer the case, and tenants are skeptical of long-term commitments in downtown areas. Of course, if the building to be leased must be extensively remodeled and these improvements are not suitable for the general run of tenants, the lease would, of necessity, have to be long term. However, if the improvements are such that they would be of benefit to almost anybody, this would have a much smaller effect on the length of the lease. Currently, leases are made downtown for as short as two or three years with options for additional years and in that way, if the tenant finds that he is successful in his downtown location, he can continue the lease.

Since these leases are not in the demand they at one time were, it is more difficult to negotiate a large amount of rental. However, profitable rentals can still be obtained. In renting a downtown building, the tenant, of course, realizes that he will have heavy traffic by his door, but he also realizes that his customers won't, in most cases, have convenient nearby parking space and that what parking spaces are available are furnished by the city or by privately owned parking facilities that charge for their use. In this way the landlord is not out anything for providing parking space as in the case of shopping centers. Since most downtown buildings are multi-story, rental for space on higher floors cannot equal the rent for ground floor space. For that reason, rental per square foot in downtown areas will generally be no greater and in some cases much less than square foot rentals in shopping centers.

COMMISSIONS AND PROFITS

To the owner of commercial property, especially downtown property, a lease is a necessity. With high property taxes, insurance rates and the possibility of vandalism, it is very expensive to keep vacant commercial property on main streets. To someone who knows where to look and who is willing to go to the work required to find a good tenant, this situation can be quite profitable. A vacant building on a main street can sometimes be picked up at a very advantageous price and leased at a figure to make a high return on the investment.

The agent can charge full commissions on leases obtained for downtown property and can find this highly profitable. In most areas, the commission amounts to 5 percent of the rent paid, and it is paid over the period of the lease. It is one of the few ways in which the real estate agent can obtain a steady regular income.

Lease Percentages

In this day of gradual inflation, a percentage of sales clause in a lease is absolutely essential. It is an unfortunate fact that some leases made many years ago, without providing for this factor, are today paying rental which does not cover the cost of taxes on the building.

The inflation protection is usually accomplished by a percentage of sales clause. The lease will state that the rent is to be paid as a percentage of sales or a fixed amount, whichever is greater. In the event of continued rising prices, the dollar sales value of the business will undoubtedly increase and will, in this way, automatically increase the rent. The percentages charged on businesses vary according to the type of business.

In the event that it is impossible to work out a lease with a sales percentage clause, the next best thing is a cost of living clause where the amount of the rent paid is adjusted according to a reliable cost of living index. When the cost of living index goes up, the rent goes up accordingly. If the tenant insists, it can also be put in the lease that if the cost of living goes down, the rent can also go down. This is a safe procedure as there is very little chance of the cost of living decreasing.

Another clause that should be put in your lease is a property tax escalation clause. Taxes get higher, and there should be some protection for the landlord. The usual way this is done is to specify that if taxes are raised after the first two years of the lease, the additional tax shall be divided between the landlord and the tenant.

POINTS TO KEEP IN MIND

- There is a future for the downtown area.
- In large cities there are separate downtown areas for different businesses.
- It is frequently rewarding to improve and upgrade old buildings.
- Many types of businesses want downtown locations, if you know how to locate them.
- Downtown leases can have attractive terms with percentage of sale clauses.

Chapter 12

Shopping Centers — The Big Money Makers

From the viewpoint of land development, the big money maker for real estate brokers and landowners today is the shopping center. Properly constructed and developed, a shopping center can be a highly profitable venture to everyone concerned. This is true of the owner, the developer, the contractor who builds, and the real estate agent who obtains leases. Frequently there will be several owners. There may be a corporate type of ownership, or it is possible that one person may own the land and another own the buildings. Type of ownership is very flexible, but properly set up, it can be very profitable.

The shopping center is an especially good income producer for a real estate agent who obtains leases. Usually leases in the shopping center will be with very strong concerns, sometimes for very large stores and usually with a long-term lease. The result is very sizable commissions for the real estate broker who acts as leasing agent.

Of course, the success or failure of the shopping center depends on how well it is planned and how well it is put together. It is our recommendation that when contemplating a shopping center, expert advisers be obtained. There should be a definite survey of the economic possibilities of any location that is considered before a final decision is made. I also recommend that a good shopping center architect be employed to draw up plans for the building. The way the shopping center is designed is very important.

A competent leasing agent should be obtained. The tenant mix in the shopping center is very important as it determines how successful the center will be. There must be enough tenants to do heavy advertising that will draw business to the center and then, after the customer gets there, there should be practically everything he wants to make a complete shopping center out of it. The tenant mix also determines the amount of financing that will be possible. The various mortgage loan companies like triple "A" leases. These are leases made by very strong concerns with triple "A" financial ratings. If you have enough of this type of lease over a long enough lease period, financing will be very easy.

SHOPPING CENTER LOCATIONS

It is certainly an established fact that the trend of the times is in favor of shopping center growth. There are a great many reasons for the growth of the shopping center, but the two main ones are convenience of parking and informality of shopping. Most shopping is done by women and a trip to the shopping center will indicate that the lady of the house has no hesitation about doing her shopping in very informal attire.

The growth in population and in the number of automobiles has led to such a congestion in the downtown areas that parking space becomes perhaps the most important single consideration in the shopping trip. There is no doubt but what the origin and growth of the shopping center has been due to this fact. Shopping centers, due to their size, location and overall layout, provide easy and convenient automobile parking.

Another advantage of the shopping center is the fact that a great number of different types of stores can be found in one location, thus making it unnecessary to walk long distances on crowded city streets to get from one type of store to another. This makes it possible to make a shopping trip during which time only one parking space need be found and yet many different types of stores are available. It makes a one-stop shopping trip with the greatest possible convenience.

The evolution of the shopping center has been from a small two- or three-acre center with a supermarket and a drug store and a variety store to the very large hundred-acre or more regional center with two or more department stores and seventy-five to one hundred smaller stores.

This trend toward shopping centers has brought many people into the shopping center business, such as land developers, real estate agents and investors. It has also led to the establishment of many thousands of branch stores of companies of all kinds. Due to the growth of the shopping center industry in recent years, there are now many thousands of them in the nation, and some localities are already finding that they have so many shopping centers that all of them cannot be profitable ventures.

The tremendous increase in the number of shopping centers has led to competition between centers, and for that reason anyone who is thinking of going into the shopping center business now needs to be very careful to see that his setup is at least equal to or better than the competition. As times goes on and people learn more about shopping centers, their development becomes more sophisticated and more experience is needed to establish a successful center.

In these days, most people have a choice of several shopping centers. Naturally they go to the one most convenient for them and the one that offers the best facilities after they get there. The most recent development in shopping centers has been the enclosed mall which is completely heated and air-conditioned inside. This seems to have an advantage over the old strip type of center and undoubtedly will take much business away from the older type of center.

HOW TO FIND THE RIGHT CITY

The growth of the shopping center has been such that some cities already have more of them than the business available justifies. However, there are a number of cities where the shopping center development has not yet reached its peak. The trend has been to extend the shopping center development to smaller communities. Until the last three or four years, it was not considered possible to put a successful shopping center in a city under about 25,000 people. Today, however, successful shopping centers are going into cities with as little as 10,000 population, especially where these cities have a considerable drawing area surrounding them.

The increase in population and especially the increase in spendable money income in the last fifteen or twenty years has made good markets of many places that were, heretofore, too small for much retail development. Actually it is possible to have a small shopping center even in a town as small as 5,000 people, although this center would be of the neighborhood type with a supermarket, drug store, a variety store, and perhaps a few smaller shops.

Size of Market

The population and income of the area to be served by a shopping center is a paramount consideration. The market must be proportionate to the size of the center that is to be developed. In order for a center to be profitable, the overall business done should exceed a minimum of sixty dollars in annual sales per square foot of building area. This figure is meaningful when applied to a reasonably complete center that has a great many different types of stores. Of course, the volume per square foot of many different types of businesses will vary from over one hundred dollars per square foot for an excellent supermarket to less than fifteen dollars per square foot for a good beauty parlor. However, with the proper tenant mix, the overall volume of the center should certainly exceed sixty dollars per square foot. For a shopping center with a retail floor area of 100,000 square feet, there must be a minimum of $6,000,000 business per year available. For this reason, the size of the market as to population and income becomes of the utmost importance. It would be very doubtful if a town of less than 10,000 people would be a suitable spot for a shopping center, unless there is an unusually large drawing area either of surrounding smaller communities or a large rural area.

Growth Factor

A consideration possibly of even more importance than the present size of the market is a question of whether it is an expanding market or a stagnant one. It is doubtful if any shopping center development could possibly be a profitable one over a period of years in a community or a market which is decreasing. It is also not desirable to have a shopping center in a market which is stagnant and which is not increasing in population and income.

Due to the fact that the overall trend of American industry in recent years has been a gradual increase in cost of doing business and a slight narrowing of profit margins, it is quite necessary that any business today have an ever increasing volume of sales. Population and income growth have made it possible for this increase in volume to take place every year in a good area. The only way that a store can successfully operate with closer profit margins and higher costs, especially labor costs, is by doing a very large volume. For this reason, it is very important that the shopping center be in a growing area.

A study of population figures of any city or market over a period of years will immediately show whether the area is growing or not. For example, some of the cities in the Appalachian coal-producing regions are steadily losing population, and the future of a shopping center development in any of these cities would be highly problematical. However, most sections of the nation are growing and it is not too difficult to find many cities which are showing a consistent upward trend.

One of the major reasons for growth in an area is its ability to attract new industry. If you know of a good live town which is working to get new industries and does have some new factories being built, the growth pattern of that area is almost assured. Another thing that you can look for is expansion in schools of higher learning. A growing college brings business to a community and helps to support a shopping center.

Generally speaking, shopping centers are divided into three classifications depending on the size and complexity of the center. The smaller center is called a neighborhood center. This is one that has a supermarket, a drug store and perhaps a variety store and three or four smaller shops such as a barber shop or beauty parlor, etc. Since the things that are sold are everyday necessities, the need for having stores of many kinds is not as keen as in the larger center. The goods sold are those that everyone has to buy and if your supermarket is a good one and you have allowed enough parking, people in convenient driving range of the center will trade there. This type of center requires a smaller population for successful operation than any other.

The next size of center is the community shopping center and is usually the largest type to be found in a city of 20,000 people or less. This shopping center, in addition to the supermarket, drug store, variety stores, etc., will have at least one medium-sized department store. It will also have a clothing store, perhaps a hardware store, paint store, shoe store and other types of smaller stores.

The largest type of center is the regional center which is only to be found in areas of large population concentration. This center, which can have a building area of up to 1,000,000 square feet or more, usually has from two to three large department stores and every conceivable type of business. Curiously enough, some of these regional centers do not have supermarkets. It is usually more convenient for the shopper to go to a smaller center for her groceries. It has been fairly well established that when people go grocery shopping, they go shopping just for that purpose alone. They do not use a grocery shopping trip to look for any other type of merchandise. For this reason, some of the very large centers do not have supermarkets. They will have usually two or three restaurants and perhaps a delicatessen, but no facilities for heavy grocery shopping.

The type of center to be built in any location depends, of course, on the population and the spendable money income of the area. An area which would be highly successful for a neighborhood shopping center might not be very good for a larger center and certainly not for a regional one.

Condition of Downtown Shopping Area

The greatest competition for any shopping center is the downtown shopping area. Do you know of a city of fair size which is growing in population and income, but has an antiquated downtown area with very little parking and very few modern stores? If so, that would be the ideal area for a shopping center. In many cities, the downtown area has not kept pace with the times. Parking is difficult if not impossible, the store fronts are completely out of date and in too many cases, the merchants are not progressive. On the other hand, if you find a downtown area that has ample parking and very modern, up-to-date and progressive merchants, your shopping center will have more difficulty getting started unless the community is large enough to support both a prosperous downtown area and shopping center.

Other Shopping Centers in Area

Since a new shopping center immediately comes in competition not only with the downtown area, but also with any other shopping centers that may be around, it is important to know the number and size of other shopping centers already established in the market. Using the figure of sixty dollars per square foot of retail area as a yardstick, is there enough business in the market to support the present shopping centers plus a new one? If there is already enough square footage in the existing shopping centers to take care of all the available business, a new center will definitely have an uphill battle. Assuming that there are 400,000 square feet of retail area in other shopping centers and the available business amounts to $24,000,000 per year, the available business justifies the present shopping centers, but does not necessarily justify a new one.

Of course, particularly in a growing area, a new and modern shopping center will frequently take business away from the older ones. In an area where there are several centers, but no mall type of center, frequently the closed mall, with its shopping comfort, will attract a great amount of business from the older centers. This is a factor that could be taken into consideration in choosing a shopping center location.

Department Stores

The big drawing card for a shopping center is a department store. Does the market which is under consideration as a location have many good department stores? If none of the shopping centers in the area under consideration has a good department store, in all probability a new center with a modern, up-to-date department store will attract much business away from the older centers. It is also important to know how many department stores are in the downtown area, and how modern, progressive and strong is their situation.

Naturally the larger and the stronger the department store, the greater the power to pull customers to the shopping center. If there are other shopping centers with small department stores, a larger and more modern one at your center may draw business away from the older shopping centers. It takes a good department store to draw the shoppers for any type of merchandise other than groceries.

HOW TO FIND A LOCATION IN THE CITY

Once an area has been picked as a suitable location for a shopping center, the exact location of the center within that market area becomes very important. This is especially true where it will compete with other existing centers and with a strong downtown area or in a market which is growing and which will be certain to attract other shopping centers in the future.

Direction of Growth

You can easily determine in any growing community the most likely direction in which growth will continue. Especially of interest is residential growth, as the shopping center should be easily available to as many homes as possible. If your center is not established in the path of growth, it is a certainty that sooner or later there will be a competing center in the growth area. For this reason, it is very important that the center be not only in an area where the present population is sufficient to support it, but in a location that can serve future population growth. It is a very good idea to visit the planning board of any city in which you are interested. Usually these boards have worked out an overall plan for future development of the area and have maps to show these plans. By looking at these maps and talking to the planning board, you can find out where they expect to zone additional property for residential building and where they expect to zone additional property for business use. Seeing the planning board and the city traffic engineer to learn about any possible new streets are both musts in choosing a shopping center location.

Traffic Patterns

The location must be such that it can be easily reached from the principal residential areas. Are there through traffic streets leading from residential areas to the vicinity of the shopping center location? Are there any collector streets that feed into the through street?

There is an advantage in having the shopping center location on a corner where it can be served by two or more streets. The ideal situation is two or more through high traffic streets which reach the general vicinity of the shopping center and then several collector streets that turn off into the actual shopping center itself. It is not a very good idea to have the actual entrance and exit of a shopping center on high speed traffic streets. Should the main entrance to the shopping center be on such a street, the cooperation of the local police department must be obtained in putting stop lights at vital points.

If the location you have under consideration is on a main highway where the maintenance is by the state highway department, it is a good idea to see the highway department and ask them for a traffic count. Not only can they usually give you an up-to-date traffic count for this highway, but frequently they can give you figures on traffic counts for other streets and areas in the city. This can be important.

New Streets and Highways

Frequently new streets and highways, especially express routes, can change the traffic pattern of a city very materially. For instance, in our city a new beltline road to completely encircle the city was planned and construction started. An enterprising developer bought a large tract of land close to the beltline with an entrance also from another major street for the purpose of a shopping center. There was very little residential development in the area and a great many people thought the shopping center would not be successful for this reason. However, with the new beltline highway in operation, it was easy for people to reach the shopping center location from almost all residential areas in the city. The shopping center turned out to be a big success, and most of the reason was the new beltline highway.

In considering any location in any given city, it is a very good idea to check with the planning board and the city traffic engineer to see what the overall plans for the traffic development are in that area. Sometimes these plans are projected so far in the future to be of very little practical use. However, you can tell by talking to various city officials how far away any planned developments might be and whether or not it is worthwhile considering them in your choice of locations.

PHYSICAL CHARACTERISTICS

A location might be in a very fine growing city and in an excellent spot within that city, but due to certain physical characteristics, might not be suitable for a shopping center.

Size

The size plot of land that will be needed will depend on the amount of business available in that area and its growth characteristics. It is nearly always advisable to have a market survey made. There are several competent firms that make these surveys and can give a reasonably accurate picture of the amount of retail business that would be available in any particular location. By arriving at the amount of retail business that you can expect, it is easy to determine what the size of the shopping center should be. If you allow sixty dollars per square foot of retail area per year, you can determine the size of the building that you should have. For example, if the survey determines that there is $18,000,000 worth of retail business available per year, you should plan on about 300,000 square feet of retail area. This is based on the assumption that you need sixty dollars per square foot of business per year. If the location is in a growth area, the amount of business will, of course, increase to where your center may be doing eighty, ninety or one hundred dollars per square foot per year in retail sales. This would make you a highly profitable center.

After the floor area you desire is determined, then the amount of parking space needed can also be determined by multiplying the amount of floor area by three. As a rule of thumb, the parking area should be three times as large as the floor area of the buildings. There is a trend recently to make the parking area three and one half to four times larger than the floor area of the building. This is especially true where buildings of more than one story are contemplated. In figuring the amount of parking area necessary, where the buildings are more than one story in height, it is necessary to calculate the floor area of the upper floors and take this area into consideration in calculating the amount of parking space. On a second or third or fourth floor, it is not necessary to figure as much as three to one parking, but about two to one is sufficient. There are advantages to having plenty of parking, because that is the primary attraction of the shopping center. There are also disadvantages to having too much parking, because it means excessive upkeep and also tends to give the center a vacant look which is very bad for business.

In going further with the illustration above where $18,000,000 of business is available and we have determined the floor area of the shopping center buildings as 300,000 square feet, the parking area should be at least three times that or 900,000 square feet, making a total area of 1,200,000 square feet. This is approximately thirty acres. If your area is a properly growing one, then you should also have some additional land for future expansion. We recommend that another twenty acres be retained for future expansion so that the overall development should plan on at least fifty acres of land. If this much area is not available, the proposed shopping center development would suffer many handicaps.

Lay of Land

Is the land reasonably level so that construction can begin without an excessive amount of grading? Sometimes a very desirable location will have such tremendous fill problems that the cost of building a shopping center in that location becomes so large as to make the project impractical. If the land is in a hollow that requires a great deal of fill, the expense of preparing it for building can be extremely high. There is also the lapse of time, as most methods of filling low land require a settling period which may delay actual construction.

Entrances and Exits

It is very advisable that the shopping center have more than one wide entrance and more than one wide exit. Preferably these exits and entrances should come from streets with comparatively slow speed traffic. It should be determined whether or not it is possible to get stop lights at the most strategic entrance. If the location fronts on a four-lane divided highway, is there a median cut so that traffic going in either direction can enter the location? If there is no median cut, what would be your chances of obtaining one? If the street in front of your location is state maintained, it would be necessary to take up this matter of median cuts with the state highway department. If it is maintained by the city, then it should be taken up with the city traffic engineer.

City Conveniences and Zoning

It will be quite necessary in your location to have city sewers and, of course, all of the utilities such as electricity, gas, etc.

Another necessity is that your property be zoned for shopping centers. The zoning required for shopping center development varies from city to city according to local custom and local law. The planning and zoning board should be consulted to find out just what the zoning is on the location. If the zoning is not proper for shopping center development, then the feasibility of getting the zoning changed should be determined. In some cities, getting the zoning changed is almost impossible and in others it is comparatively easy. An attorney who is well acquainted with the planning board will be of a great deal of service to you in the event that a zone change is necessary.

In many cities there will be a great deal of opposition to getting any zone change for the purpose of putting in a shopping center. This opposition will come from downtown merchants, other shopping center developers, and in some cases, nearby homeowners who do not want commercial development in their area.

I know of cases in my home town where shopping center developers have purchased land only to see it sit idle for as long as five to ten years because of the inability to get it zoned due to the opposition of other commercial interests in the community.

OWNERSHIP

Ownership of the land which is suitable for shopping center locations is very important. Often the ownership of the land will determine whether or not it can be used for a shopping center and, of course, the question of whether or not the land is for sale or lease is important.

Individual or Corporate

Is the land owned by an individual or by a corporation? If it is owned by an individual, are they interested in selling or leasing? If it is owned by a corporation, the probabilities are that it is owned with the idea of some future development on the part of the present owners. Perhaps the land is owned by an estate or trust. If that is the case, it might be very difficult to get the cooperation of the owners either in selling or leasing or in helping in the development. Especially if the land is entailed where the present owners cannot sell it or cannot do anything with it, then the prospects of actually using the land for commercial development may be impossible.

It is a very good idea for the prospective shopping center developer to look up the deed to the land as recorded in the courthouse and see if there are any restrictions on its use. This should be done even before talking to the owner.

Frequently in a deed, you will find restrictions of various kinds as to the use of the land. Perhaps some owner along the line was a prohibitionist and there may be a restriction in the deed against the sale of liquor on that particular land. This is one of the most common restrictions found, but there are others which might be present. All this must be taken into consideration when choosing a location.

Will the Owner Cooperate?

Does the owner want to sell and get out of the ownership entirely or does he want to cooperate with a proposed shopping center developer? If either one of these is true, undoubtedly something can be worked out, provided the price and terms are within reason.

PRICE AND TERMS OF THE LAND

What is the value of the land under its present use? How much additional value would be created by putting a shopping center on it? It is generally considered that a shopping center developer can pay $15,000 an acre or, in good places, considerably more than that. The matter of the proper value of the land can probably be determined by having it appraised by a local appraiser or by comparing sales of comparable land in the vicinity which have been made recently.

If it is determined that the land can be purchased for a reasonable sum, on what terms can it be purchased? The purchase of a large tract of land for both present and future development can sometimes require a very large amount of cash. It is not desirable to tie up much cash for what may be a long period of development and construction. For that reason, it is important to know how the owner will cooperate in selling it. Will the owner give an option on the entire tract and allow the developer to exercise the option a little at a time? In this case, all the developer actually needs to buy is the land he needs for the initial phase of his construction and then as the project expands, he can exercise options on additional parts. This makes it possible to proceed with a minimum of cash working capital.

Owner As a Partner with the Developer

Frequently the owner is interested in putting in his land as part ownership of the shopping center. In this case, it should be a corporate structure with the landowner obtaining enough shares of stock to compensate him for the value of his land. In the event that the owner owns his land free and clear without any mortgages on it, this is a very desirable way to proceed and will require a minimum of cash investment on the part of the developer.

Frequently the owner will wish to do all of the building and construction and be sole owner of the shopping center himself. With the proper tenants and sensible construction of the center, the owner, if he has his land free and clear, can usually build without any investment other than the land itself, as he can usually obtain mortgage financing for the total cost of the construction. It has been possible for financing to be obtained to cover both the cost of the land and the development. This is not the case today though, as mortgage lenders are more prudent than they have been in the past. However with the proper mix of tenants where a large portion of them are triple "A" concerns, very advantageous financing can be obtained.

POINTS TO KEEP IN MIND

- *Location.* This is extremely important and should be carefully considered as to area served and what streets and highways are nearby.
- *How to find the right city.* It is important that the shopping center be in a city that is growing and that needs this type of shopping area.
- *Finding locations in the city.* After finding that a particular city is a good one for shopping center development, then it is necessary to find suitable location within the city by considering direction of growth, traffic patterns, streets and highways, etc.
- *Physical characteristics of location.* They should be suitable for a shopping center, and such considerations as size, lay of land, entrances and exits and proper zoning are very important.
- *Ownership.* Before any efforts can be made to start developing a shopping center, it is necessary to determine who the owners will be.

Chapter 13

How to Organize Shopping Center Development for Successful Completion in the Least Possible Time

After a suitable location has been found, the work of building a shopping center has just begun. In order to make possible the development of a shopping center, some form of organization must be arranged. The successful completion of a good shopping center in a reasonable length of time will depend on how well the development organization is set up. The important considerations are the personnel in the organization, the capital requirements, the proper contracts between the parties and the skill and experience of the professional advisers that should be employed.

WHEN OWNER OF LAND WANTS TO BE OWNER OF COMPLETED CENTER

There are definite advantages to owning a shopping center. If properly set up and with the proper leases, it can be highly profitable. Also the factor of depreciation on the buildings will cause income taxes for a long time to be very low.

Another advantage to an owner of the land becoming owner of the shopping center is the fact that frequently the financial arrangements can be very easily made. This is true if the owner owns the land outright without any mortgage on it. Frequently the land itself is all the equity needed, and all of the rest of the money needed to develop and build the shopping center can be obtained on a long-term mortgage. With the near certainty of continued gradual inflation and continual gradual erosion of the dollar, the payments on the mortgage will probably be made in cheaper dollars than was the case when the original mortgage was made.

Necessity for Professional Developers

With the competition which any new shopping center will have from the downtown central shopping district and from other shopping centers in the area, it is necessary that the center be developed in a professional and sophisticated manner. With the many new shopping centers drawing business away from the downtown area, downtown merchants in many cities are fighting back by upgrading their downtown stores and, in cooperation with city officials, creating many new parking lots and parking spaces. The developers of a new shopping center must take all of this competition into consideration in arranging their layout.

Overall Architectural Layout

There are many architects who have had experience and who specialize in making shopping center plans. By all means, if the center is any larger than a neighborhood one, an experienced architect should be retained. The architects will take such important things into consideration as adequate parking and traffic flow, as well as plans and specifications for the actual building.

Building Contractor

The contractor who is engaged to do the actual building is a very important cog in the shopping center development machinery. His experience and ability should be such that he can carry out the architectural plans efficiently and at a reasonable cost. It is also important that the contractor be financially sound, so that there will be no interruptions in his work during the construction period. The builder should be one that has a reputation for carrying his jobs through promptly. The shorter the construction time, the less the capital costs of building the center because of the interest saved on borrowed money.

Leasing Agent

Since the income of the shopping center comes from rentals received from tenants, it is very important that the leases be the best obtainable. For this reason it is essential that the developers have a professional leasing agent. This agent should be familiar with the various chains throughout the country and if he has had experience, will personally know many of the officials of the companies. He should also be familiar with the terms usually acceptable to the various companies and with the amount of rental which the different types of retail concerns can afford to pay.

DUTIES OF DEVELOPER

The duty of a developer is to start with a raw piece of land and end up with a completed and profitable shopping center.

Planning Stage

The first thing a developer must do is set up an overall plan for the development of the center. By using the feasibility study of the market which he has undoubtedly had made by a good survey firm before choosing the location, he can determine the size of the shopping center. Once having determined the size of the center, he can then decide on the method of construction to be used. If the center is a very small one, it can be a strip center; otherwise it might be advisable to make a mall type of center. Much would depend on the competition from the downtown area and from other shopping centers. The main consideration is to have a modern center with drawing power that can survive the competition in the area.

The next step in the planning operation would be to consult with the architect as to the plan and layout of the center. With the developer's knowledge of the requirements of various types of firms and with the architect's knowledge of shopping centers and buildings, a plan can be worked out with logical locations for each type of store. Frequently the exact size of the various stores cannot be determined until at least some of the leases have been made. However, the location of the supermarket and the department store and other types of stores can be determined to some degree.

At this time also the cost of operating the center should be considered. The cost of maintaining the center will depend to some extent on the initial planning which goes into its layout. The maintenance problems of shopping centers are primarily that of keeping the parking area and the other common areas clean and free from ice and snow. In some northern areas, the question of snow and ice removal becomes one of the largest cost of operation. Other costs of operation are taxes, about which very little can be done, and insurance. The insurance rates can be reduced to a minimum by sound construction of the center.

Leases

The developer should oversee the operations of the leasing agent and check to be sure that the highest possible rentals are being obtained and that the leases obtained fit into the general overall layout of the center.

Building Construction

The developer should also oversee the building contractor and, with the cooperation of the architect, see that specifications are met and that the various storerooms are built in the size and manner required by the lessees.

Necessity for Long-Term Contract

It always takes longer to complete a shopping center than any of the parties anticipate. The planning stage always takes longer than expected and should not be cut short, because it should be very carefully done. Before the building actually starts, it is usually advisable to get leases from the largest tenants so that the storerooms can be designed to their specifications. The negotiation of these leases is sometimes a very slow process. Theoretically, it should be very simple to make a lease with a chain store for any particular location. However, the big companies are so besieged by requests from their district managers and regional managers for additional stores and so deluged with literature from would-be shopping center developers that it takes a long time to get the attention of the proper people. Even after their attention has been obtained, the chain will usually make a survey of the area before determining whether or not they are interested. After their interest is once obtained, it becomes the question of negotiating the lease. Since the average chain store lease form will cover several closely typewritten pages, sometimes it takes a surprisingly long time to work out a lease which is satisfactory to the tenant and the developers and owners of the shopping center.

Due to the long time involved in completing a shopping center, the contract with the developers certainly would have to be for a long period of time also. It can usually be figured that the time for building a moderate-sized center from the time the location is selected would have to be several years. In fact, from the developer's standpoint, the contract should run far enough to take care of future expansion after the original shopping center itself is built. There is nearly always a time a few years after the shopping center opens when it becomes desirable to add additional space. This is the case when the shopping center is a profitable one. If the development has been planned properly and the proper leases have been obtained, the center will be a profitable one and probably will be expanded, and the contract should run from ten to fifteen years, to be sure to cover all contingencies.

Advantages to Developer or Agent

The gains by the developer or agent are of a great deal of importance. Probably no other field of real estate endeavor is any more profitable to a real estate agent or shopping center developer.

Probably the most obvious advantage is the size of the development. The amount of money that a developer or a real estate agent can make through developing a good shopping center will probably be far more than he could expect to gain in the usual routine operation of a real estate office. The cost of the center can vary from one to fifteen or twenty million dollars or more for the very large ones, and the income from it can also run into a very large amount of money.

The remuneration to the developer can be in cash or it can be by his getting a part interest in the shopping center without the investment of any capital. In either event, it is very worthwhile.

Another advantage to the developer or agent is that if he makes one good shopping center that is profitable to the owners and successful from the viewpoint of the merchants in it, he will have a demand for his services for other centers. There is really no limit to how far he can go on this or how big an operation he can have in developing shopping centers. Shopping center development is a career in itself and at this time in the growth of the country, a very important one.

WHAT AGENT MUST KNOW BEFORE ENTERING INTO CONTRACT

Since the developer or agent is planning to put a great deal of time and a certain amount of expense into the operation, he must satisfy himself that the possibilities of the successful completion of a good shopping center are in his favor. For this reason, he must be thoroughly familiar with certain points, such as the feasibility of the location and the market potential such as would be brought out in the feasibility survey. Other aspects that he must be familiar with are:

Financial Condition of the Owner

This is very important as sometimes developers of shopping centers will work very hard getting the shopping center started, only to find that the owner is unable to complete building of the center due to inadequate finances. It is important to check whether or not the land is free and clear of all mortgages. The financial reputation and ability of the owner should be checked and if good, about all he needs is the land free and clear. However, this is a matter of a great deal of importance to the agent and developer and should be very carefully investigated.

Cooperation of Owner

It is also important to know that the developer will be allowed to proceed in a realistic and professional manner. The best possible contract is one where the developer has absolute authority to build and obtain leases and everything necessary to make a successful center. If the owner balks at this kind of contract and wants some provision by which all major decisions must in the final analysis be made by him, then the owner must be very carefully investigated further. Is he a type that cooperates in a business-like manner, or is he someone who procrastinates or wants to run things even though he does not know how to go about it? Sometimes an owner will feel, since he is the owner of the shopping center, that he should be consulted on all matters and that he should build the center the way he wants it built. The usual owner really does not know anything about shopping center construction or layout or shopping center leases and can frequently be very much of a stumbling block to the developer.

WHEN OWNER WANTS TO BE ACTIVE DEVELOPER

Whether or not the active participation of the owner is a good thing or not depends on the owner. If he is a good businessman and has time to devote to the project, it can be worked out to be a very advantageous arrangement for everyone concerned.

Advantages to Owner

The advantages to the owner of active participation in the development of the project are several. There is, of course, the pride of accomplishment which is a matter of personal satisfaction and a very worthwhile consideration. Also by taking an active part in the development of the shopping center, the owner can oversee the activities of the various agents and satisfy himself that they are doing a good job. He can check on them and, if there is anything that he thinks can be improved, he is in a position to make suggestions and carry through and see that the improvements are made.

The owner's interest is somewhat different from the interest of his agents in that the owner is primarily concerned with the profitability of the center after it is finished. Sometimes factors that affect the ultimate profitability of the operation are overlooked by the agents, not intentionally, but because their interest is just not quite as strong as the owner's. By active participation, the owner can watch out for such points as the profitability of leases, lower operating expenses on the center, etc.

In virtually every case of building a shopping center, financial arrangements play an important part. By taking an active part in the development, the owner can be sure that his financial position is not overextended. This is important as, should it become necessary to put up more cash than was originally planned, it might be of some embarrassment and some difficulty to the owner. By being familiar with the day-to-day activities as well as the overall plan of the development, the owner can protect himself, not only as to ultimate profitability of the center, but as to the effect on his immediate finances so that he will run no risk of becoming overextended.

Advantages to Agent

Where the owner takes an active part in the development, frequently the principal activity of the agent would be in securing good tenants for the center. In this capacity, he would be primarily a leasing agent. There are a number of advantages to the agent in confining his activities to leasing. It means that he has less authority, but also less responsibility. It also means that he has smaller expense of operation and has fewer dollars and hours of his time invested before commissions are earned.

Commissions are usually paid over the term of the lease and are about the only way that the usual real estate broker can obtain a steady consistent income. Many of the leases will be for fifteen years or more and will provide an income for the agent for that length of time. It is true that while the leases are being obtained, the agent has expenses to bear without any income coming in. However, once the center has been completed and the tenants are paying rent, his income becomes regular with hardly any expense and what he takes in is almost all profit.

If the center is very large, sometimes the income derived from it is sufficient to give the broker a very excellent income for a long period of time.

Need for Exclusive Contract

In order to assure close and continuous cooperation between the leasing agent and the active developing owner, an exclusive contract for the leasing agent is a necessity. From the owner's viewpoint, it makes one person responsible for obtaining leases and reporting to him about them. It avoids any possibility of arguments with various real estate brokers as to who obtained what leases. It nearly always happens, where there is no exclusive contract, that more than one broker will show the same property to the same prospects, and then there is a conflict of interest as to who obtained the lease and who is entitled to the commission. This creates a nuisance for the developing owner, and he can avoid it very simply by exclusive contract with one good leasing agent.

By having an exclusive contract with one agent, it assures the owner that he will have an agent who will take a great deal of interest in the property, do his best to obtain good leases and work consistently on the project. Where there is no one with exclusive contract, there is no one responsible for obtaining leases and no one will take anything like as much interest as someone who does have the exclusive contract.

From the broker's standpoint, the advantages of exclusive contract are obvious. A great many centers are very difficult to start, but once a large and prominent tenant has been obtained, the other and smaller tenants come along rather automatically. The agent may work for two years getting the proper lease from their number one department store tenant, and certainly he deserves to be able to make the other and smaller and easier leases. By having only one exclusive agent, the agent can understand the situation. He knows the provisions of the leases and will not waste time trying to get prospects that could not go in the center anyway due to conflict with other leases, and he is also more interested in getting the proper tenant mix.

Good Situation for a Real Estate Broker

One of the best jobs which the real estate broker can obtain is as leasing agent for a shopping center, provided the location is good and the developer, whether he be owner or someone else, has the necessary financing to complete the center. A great deal, of course, also depends on whether or not the developers are willing to employ competent architects and builders to construct the center.

The resulting commissions from getting good tenants for shopping centers will over a period of years run into a very considerable amount of money and make a very significant addition to the broker's income. The commissions usually charged will vary anywhere from 2 to 4 percent of the actual rentals. Some of these contracts call for paying the commission quarterly and some semiannually on the basis of the rents collected in the previous three or six months, as the case may be. Sometimes contracts are written where the commissions are paid in advance, every three months on the rentals expected in the following three months. This usually requires an adjustment from each period to another, and it is more difficult to keep the proper records and thus, is not a very good or desirable method of doing it. The best way is to have the leases paid after the rental is paid, and in that way there is no question as to the amount of money due the broker as commission.

WHEN OWNER WANTS TO SELL

Sometimes the owner wants to sell the land outright and in that case it is necessary for the developer to buy it, provided he is financially able, or if not, he would have to obtain some other form of financing. In this situation where the land has to be purchased by someone to develop it, there are several important points to consider.

Price

The cost of the land on which the shopping center is to be built is a very important item. It usually becomes a capital investment and since the land cannot be depreciated for income tax purposes, the cost of it cannot be recovered through depreciation.

After assessing the location and looking over the feasibility study for the area and deciding what size shopping center should be built in that location, then a projection of earnings should be made. For an income for the center, as a rough rule of thumb, you can use $1.90 per square foot for the building area as annual rental. If the building area is 200,000 square feet, you can say the gross income of the center is about $380,000. This figure must be sufficient to cover expenses of operation of the center, plus interest on the mortgage and the required payments on it. By making a projected profit and loss statement for the center, using the rough rule of thumb as an income basis, it is possible to obtain an idea as to whether the center will be profitable. If it appears it will be, you can decide whether or not it will amount to some sort of reasonable interest return on the actual amount of cash invested. It is usually possible to obtain fairly close figures as to construction costs from a reliable builder in the locality. On the basis of the price of the land and the building cost, it is possibile to determine the property tax and the insurance cost. You can also estimate the cost of the upkeep of the center in terms of keeping it clean and in keeping the outside of the buildings in repair. You should add in the cost of the leasing agent's commission and any other logical expenses that could arise. If this protection of earnings is realistically done, it can be very close to what will happen in actual practice.

Terms

Another important consideration is the terms on which the owner of the land is willing to sell. The better the terms, the less capital investment is required. Sometimes the land on which the actual building is to be built can be purchased, with a long-term option on adjoining land which you might need in the future for expansion. This is a very advantageous way to handle the matter as it requires a tie up of a smaller amount of actual cash capital.

Getting a Financial Backer

The most essential requirement for the financial backer is, of course, that he have enough money. Usually enough money to purchase the land for cash without any mortgage on it is about all that is necessary if the location is a good one and the plan for the shopping center is sound.

It may be that the financial backer can be interested only as a financial arrangement without taking any active part in the development, or he can be someone who wishes to take an active part in planning and building the shopping center. As mentioned previously in this chapter, if he does wish to be active in the development, it is necessary to screen him carefully to see that he is a good businessman and does have time enough to devote to developing this center.

In finding a financial backer, probably the best way to proceed is through acquaintances or friends of the agent who wishes to develop the shopping center. Of course, if the agent has enough money of his own to do it, then there is no problem, but such is usually not the case. By inquiring among his friends and acquaintances, he can usually line up several potential financial backers.

After getting a list of potential financial backers, it becomes necessary to sell at least one of them on the idea of purchasing the land and building a shopping center. Here is where the projected earnings statement, which should be conservatively figured to show a reasonable return on the actual cash investment, makes a very excellent presentation to the prospective financial backer. It should be explained to the prospective backer that the leases will all have percentage of sales clauses in them and, if the center is as successful as expected, these percentage of sales clauses will come into effect. The best profits from shopping centers do occur where the tenant pays a percentage override. If the guaranteed portion of the rental is enough to give a reasonable income on the cash investment, usually the center will have proved over a period of time to be a very profitable one for the owner due to the percentage of sales clauses in the leases.

Forming a Corporation

In the event that an individual financial backer is not desired or can't be found, the capital requirements can frequently be met by forming a corporation with several stockholders. In this way it is not necessary for any one individual to put up large sums of money. From the practical standpoint of developing the center, it is desirable to have as few stockholders as possible due to the resulting ease in handling the corporation. Sometimes the agent who wants to develop the center will take a sizable interest himself in cash, or he might take his remuneration for developing the center in stock in the corporation and become a sizable owner of the completed shopping center in this manner.

In the event that there are a large number of small shareholders, it is probably advantageous for the developer to be elected president of the corporation so that he will be responsible for its operation. It might be considered an advantage to have one of the stockholders a good building contractor since, as part owner of the center, he might give extra attention and extra efficiency to actually constructing the buildings in the center.

WHEN OWNER OF LAND WANTS A PART INTEREST IN THE SHOPPING CENTER

There are some cases in which the owner of the land would like to have a part interest in the shopping center but does not feel that he wants to make the investment necessary to be the sole owner. There are several methods in which the owner of the land can contribute to the development of the shopping center through part interest.

Usually when the land owner wants a part interest in the shopping center, it is necessary to form a corporation. The owner can then pay cash for some of the shares of stock, or he can sell the land and take payment of half of it in cash and the other half in stock in the corporation. Sometimes the owner will deposit all of his land for an interest in the corporation with the understanding that the value of his land will be met by cash from other stockholders. This is the usual way of doing it.

In the event that the owner does contribute his part of the capital of the developing corporation by putting in part or all of his land, it is important to have a sound professional appraisal of the land value. The owner of the land should not be allowed a greater interest in the corporation than the actual value of his land at the time the corporation is formed.

It is possible that a partnership could be formed with the agent or developer putting up money and the landowner putting up land. Here again, it is necessary to make a fair appraisal of the value of the land at the time the organization is formed.

In any event, there should be a detailed contract between the landowner and the developing corporation or the developing agent, as the case may be. This contract should cover such things as the accepted value of the land, what proportion of the developing corporation the landowner is to get, whether or not he is to take an active part in the development work and what part the agent is responsible for and, in fact, the contract should be detailed enough to cover practically all of the details that can arise.

POINTS TO KEEP IN MIND

Due to the competition for retail business today, it is important that the shopping center development be properly organized. The type of organization will depend on who is the owner of the property.

- If the owner of the land wants to be owner of the completed center, he must be sold on the advantages of having professional developers, good architectural layout, a good building contractor and leasing agent.
- The duties of the developer will cover about everything, but should include the planning for the center, obtaining leases, building construction, etc.
- Before entering into the contract, the agent, to protect himself, must know the financial condition of the owner and how much cooperation he can expect from him.
- If the owner wants to be an active developer, there are certain

advantages and disadvantages to his being active and actually developing the property of the shopping center. An important consideration is to write a suitable contract which covers all contingencies.

- If the owner wants to sell, a different type of organization is needed. The important thing to consider is how much the owner is going to charge for the land, on what terms he is going to sell it and whether or not the developer has either the finances necessary himself or can acquire them. Frequently forming a corporation is the answer.

Chapter 14

What a Profitable Shopping Center Must Provide

The ultimate goal and reason for building a shopping center is, of course, to make profit. In order for a shopping center to be profitable, it must attract a great many customers, so that the tenants in the center will do a sufficient volume of business. The profitable shopping center must not only have basic guaranteed rentals, but must have sales overrides. The amount of the sales override depends, of course, on the total sales of the various tenants in the center. In order for these tenants to attract enough customers to enable them to make sufficient sales to pay overrides as well as to show a profit, the center must have certain features. In the long run, the prosperity of the shopping center will depend upon the prosperity of the tenants in it. The interest of the developer of the shopping center and of the tenants in it are very much the same—a large volume of business is required by everyone. There has been a tendency for the cost of doing business to increase and in order to offset these increases, a constant increase in volume of business must take place. The accent today is on a high volume of business in order to counteract more intense competition and higher operating costs.

CONVENIENCE OF LOCATION

Obviously, the easier it is for people to reach the center, the more of them are going to do so. The location must primarily be one where there are people with spendable money income. The type and size of center will depend to a large extent on how many people are in the area and how they are located. Are these people concentrated in a comparatively small area or are they scattered over a very wide area making it necessary for them to drive a long way in order to get to the center?

Convenient Type of Shopping Center

If the plan is to build a convenient type of shopping center which will have a supermarket, a drug store, a variety store and a few other smaller tenants, it is obviously of advantage for the population to be in a small compact area. The merchandise carried in the convenient type of center is primarily that which is purchased by people every day or at least very often, and the closer these people live to the center, the more often they will use its facilities. The stores in the convenient center can include a beauty parlor and a barber shop. In general, the types of stores in this center are those where the average shopper does not feel it necessary to compare prices on items in other stores, and where the purchases are comparatively small so that it does not seem necessary to travel a long distance to obtain the desired items. This is certainly typified by the supermarket and the drug store. The people coming to the drug store and supermarket should, if the center is laid out properly, pass the variety store, as there are a lot of items in the variety store which are impulse purchases. Other stores visited frequently are, of course, laundry pickups, dry cleaners, etc.

Stores such as beauty shops and barber shops are places that are visited specifically for the purpose of obtaining the service rendered. It isn't very often that a man goes on a shopping tour and incidentally while shopping gets a haircut. He usually goes to a certain area for the expressed purpose of getting a haircut and does not do much shopping while on the same trip. The same thing is true of the beauty parlor operation.

Neighborhood Shopping Center

The neighborhood shopping center is somewhat larger than the convenient type of shopping center and must draw more people. Frequently in a small or medium-sized town, the only shopping center will be of the neighborhood type. This type of shopping center, in addition to the stores usually found in the convenient type of shopping center, will also have a department store and several other businesses not usually found in the convenient type, such as hardware stores, bakeries, clothing stores of various kinds, appliance stores, etc.

Due to the larger number of stores in the neighborhood center, there must be more money spent to support these stores, and it is necessary to attract customers from a somewhat wider area. In the neighborhood center, it is more important to have good access streets, preferably thruways, approaching the center, so the people can reach it from a wider area.

Regional Centers

These centers are the largest type of center and are designed to appeal to a great many people. Usually the regional type of center will have two or more large department stores and several women's clothing stores, several men's clothing stores and as many as 100 to 120 small merchants. Obviously these centers must attract a great many people to provide the necessary sales volume to support the center and make the tenants in it profitable, and also to make the development profitable for the developers.

The regional type of center must not only draw from the immediate market area, but also from distant areas. In some instances, the regional type of center will draw from other towns as far away as twenty or thirty miles or even farther. For that reason, it must supply just about everything that a shopper would expect to find anywhere. The average shopper, a great majority of which are women, like to compare prices and items. For this reason, there must be several stores of each type. The average woman shopper will not buy any sizable item without visiting two or three stores and comparing the quality and design of the products and prices.

Due to the fact the regional center must draw from a wide area, the location is very important, especially in relation to highways leading to the immediate vicinity. It should have through traffic arteries, four lanes or more that come from various parts of the area from which the center expects to draw.

PARKING

The outstanding reason for the success of the shopping center has been convenient parking. The ever increasing traffic congestion in urban areas and the lack of good high speed mass transport, has led to a strong need for a shopping area with convenient parking. This is what the shopping center should and must provide.

Size and Layout

The size of the parking area must be in proportion to the size of the retail shopping area. By modern standards, the size of the parking area should have, expressed in square footage, at least three times the area of the retail floor space in the buildings in the center. Some shopping centers have from three and a half to four times the area in parking, and many times this is an advantage. It is difficult to increase the amount of parking space once the parking lot has been designed, so it is probably a good idea today to plan for about three and a half times the retail area.

By way of illustration, in a neighborhood center of 60,000 square feet of retail building area, the parking lot should be about 210,000 square feet or an overall shopping center area of 270,000 square feet. For a larger neighborhood center with perhaps 200,000 square feet of retail floor space, the parking lot should be about 700,000 square feet or a total square footage of about 900,000 square feet or approximately 20 acres. For the regional type of center, the size would still be in proportion.

Some of the parking area will necessarily be used by employees of the various businesses in the center. Parking must be available, otherwise space will be taken by employees' cars that is needed by shoppers who visit the center. The employees' cars stay at the center all day long, and each car occupies one space continuously all day long. It is estimated that the turnover in parking spaces is from six to eight times per day, depending on the time spent in the center by the average shopper. This means that each employee's car is actually taking up space that could be used by six to eight customers. For this reason, it is a good idea to have the employee in the least valuable parking spaces. In the strip type of center, this will usually be in the rear of the buildings. In the mall center, employee parking should be as far away as possible from the major entrances to the mall. After setting aside certain spaces for employees, the question of getting the employees to use these spaces and seeing that they do is a problem for the merchant's association of the center and each employer.

Each space in the parking lot should be indicated by white lines.

The layout must provide sufficient drives, free of parking, so that there is no problem about reaching parking spaces once the customer is actually in the parking lot. There seems to be some difference of opinion as to whether the parking spaces should be parallel to, vertical to or diagonal to the actual shopping center buildings. Most park diagonally with the driveways running vertical to the actual buildings. In this event, the driveways should be indicated as to direction flow by arrows painted on the surface of the parking lot. Every other driveway should go in one direction, and every other driveway in the other.

Needless to say the attractiveness of the shopping center is important in getting the required number of shoppers and customers. For this reason it is a good idea to plan for landscaping in the parking lot. This can be done by shrubbery around some of the lighting posts or shrubbery around the edges of the buildings, but certainly there should be some effort to relieve the barren monotony of the concrete or blacktop surface. In connection with the construction of the parking lot, a concrete parking lot is more expensive in the first place but requires less maintenance. Most parking lots are blacktop, which requires retopping from time to time.

One of the very important things to take into consideration in laying out a parking lot is lighting it. Almost always, shopping centers stay open after dark and in many of them, the largest business is done in the evening hours. For this reason sufficient lighting is an absolute necessity.

A lighting engineer should be consulted as to the placement of the lightposts and the amount of light that each should require. The lighting engineer can design the posts in such a way that there will be no dark spots and no shadows, and the parking lot will be completely lighted.

Ingress and Egress

In most cases, the design and location of the entrances and exits to the center will be determined in very large measure by the surrounding streets or by the center. Is this street a four lane divided high speed highway? Is it a narrow neighborhood street, or is there a combination of two or three different kinds? If the main entrance to the center must be on a four lane divided high speed road, it is necessary to have a stoplight at the main entrance or, in the case of a large center, stoplights at two or three or more entrances. It is also important to get the highway department's cooperation in making median cuts so that traffic can turn right or left into the center. If this is necessary, it is also very helpful to have left turn loading lanes. In most cases, the highway department will cooperate in this matter, since it is also to their interest.

If there are several streets that go by or lead to the center, as is usually the case in a large or regional type of center, there can be entrances from two or more streets. If some of these streets are narrow, neighborhood streets without a great deal of traffic, a stoplight is usually not needed.

The entrances and exits should be plainly marked so that there will be no confusion on the part of anyone entering or leaving the center. Also the speed limit for cars after entering the center should be plainly indicated, and there must be a definite endeavor to see that speed limits are observed.

Once cars have entered the center, the traffic file lanes as indicated previously should be so plainly marked that the shopper will have no difficulty in determining which way to go to find a parking space. In the case of very large centers, where the parking lot is extremely large there is always the shopper who leaves his or her car on the lot and then when through shopping is unable to find it. In these very large parking lots it is sometimes helpful to designate some six, eight or ten different parking areas. These areas can be differentiated by signs placed on the light poles in different colors. Section A of the parking lot might be in red, section B in blue, etc. In this case if the customer can remember the area of the shopping center in which he is parked and also the color, he will have no difficulty in finding it, as the signs are usually placed high so that they can be seen from a distance over the tops of cars.

Enforcing Traffic and Parking Regulations

The various driving lanes must be kept clear of parking so as to provide uninterrupted traffic flow. Sometimes this proposes a problem, especially in the lane next to the building itself. It is surprising how many people will pull up directly by the store that they wish to visit and pull into the curb and park even though the area is plainly marked, "no parking." The question of how to stop the various parking infractions is a very ticklish one in many centers. However, it must be enforced and in the larger centers, there are uniformed special police who handle this situation.

TENANT DRAWING POWER

Drawing power is important for any size and type of shopping center. By drawing power, I mean that it must have the type of stores in which people like to buy and where they will go to purchase merchandise. This drawing power is important due to the competition of other shopping centers and the downtown area, and it is absolutely necessary to attract enough sales volume to the center to make the various merchants operate in a profitable manner. If the various tenants operate in a profitable manner, the owner and developer of the shopping center will also show profit. If enough business is obtained at the center, the sales override clauses in leases will come into effect. The extra rentals collected through sales overrides do not increase the expense of operating the center at all, and are therefore carried through in their entirety to net profit for the operation.

Another important reason why there must be tenant drawing power is due to the smaller stores in the center. There are few small local merchants who can draw trade from a large area by themselves. They need the traffic generated by people coming to the larger store that draws more people from larger areas.

Convenient Type of Center

In a convenient type of center, the key tenants are supermarket, drug store and variety store. Any of the national chain supermarkets have a great deal of drawing power and do heavy advertising. In some areas there will be a strong regional chain that is more popular locally than any of the nationals. In this event it is probably better to have the strong regional chain, provided their lease is strong enough to be used in financing the center. Obtaining the largest possible mortgage on the best possible terms is usually a very important consideration in the choice of tenants. The large nationwide, financially strong supermarket chains are excellent from the financing viewpoint. The two important aspects—the necessity of financing and the popularity of the particular store locally—must be balanced to determine which supermarket you would prefer to have.

As for the drug store, here again the first question is between a chain and a local druggist. The financing question enters into this frequently. If there is a large chain that is interested in coming into the area, one that has a very strong financial backing and is popular with local people, that would be your first choice. If the area is such that there are no chain stores interested, then the only thing to do is get the most popular local druggist. Frequently various wholesale drug firms will cosign leases for local druggists who agree to buy a certain proportion of their supplies from the wholesaler. This method of procedure can often solve the financing problem for a popular local druggist. A number of wholesalers are triple "A" rated and are just as strong on the lease as a national chain.

The variety store usually poses a problem, as there are not many national companies expanding in the variety store business. The City Products Company, owners of Ben Franklin Stores, Scott Stores and some other variety chains are the most active ones in most areas. There are also smaller regional or local chains that are strong in their particular home areas. Here again the question of financing becomes an important consideration. It is rather difficult to find a variety store, either chain or local, that can afford to pay the rental that you are able to obtain from other firms. This is a very difficult part of the convenient type of centers, and is frequently omitted entirely from the center.

The important point about the smaller tenants in the center is that they conduct good businesses, have reasonably good financial ratings and are popular locally. Frequently you can get a barber shop where the barber has a following already built up in the community and who will bring a certain number of people to the shopping center. The same thing is even more true of beauty parlors. Many of these shops have followings from women who have been availing themselves of their service for many years and will follow them wherever they go. By getting one of these beauty parlor operators, you not only are more secure that you have a tenant who will be a profitable operator, but you will also bring people to your center who might buy other things while they are there.

In the neighborhood center the principal tenant would be a medium-sized department store. Nearly all of the large variety chains, such as Woolworth, Grant, Kresge, etc., are opening department stores instead of the older variety store. Since these department stores carry all the merchandise formerly carried by variety stores, as well as a great many other things, it is not necessary to have a variety store in the center where there is one of these stores. These department stores are usually very aggressive advertisers and, since they present a well-known name to the shoppers, they will inevitably draw quite a number of shoppers to the center. These firms are all well-rated financially and are good from the viewpoint of financing the center.

The neighborhood center should have a strong supermarket and a drug store and about anything else that a person would buy where they do not particularly look for comparison shopping. The neighborhood center will undoubtedly have two, three or four clothing stores, one or two shoe stores plus other smaller tenants.

There should also be at least one good restaurant. Frequently the department store will have a restaurant in connection with its operation. The restaurant is needed so that shoppers who arrive late in the morning do not have to go home to get lunch, but can stay in the center. The restaurant, if a good one, will also draw additional business to the shopping center.

Regional Center

The regional center which offers about everything for sale that is found in the usual downtown area will usually have two department stores, one with higher quality merchandise and the other with somewhat lower prices. Sometimes there are more than two department stores in the very big regional center. In order to draw people from far away in sufficient numbers, the center must offer just about everything you can find of interest to a shopper.

Needless to say the strength of the department stores will largely determine the success of the center. These stores must be very strong to draw enough people to take care of the smaller specialty tenants. In these regional centers, there would be many small stores, clothing, shoes, hardware, service stores and even some offices. None of these stores is usually strong enough to draw enough business to the center to enable them to have a profitable operation. They must have the traffic coming to the big department stores and passing by their windows to generate sufficient business to make them profitable and good rent payers.

SHOPPING COMFORT

With the intense competition in businesses today among shopping centers, shopping areas and downtown areas, comfort of shopping is a very important consideration.

The Mall

The trend in recent years has been toward the enclosed mall type of center. The primary reason for this has been the comfort and ease of shopping where all stores are under one roof and are independent of weather conditions. The entire mall is heated and air-conditioned and, regardless of the temperature or whether or not it is raining or snowing outside, people can shop in perfect comfort.

Other advantages of the mall are that after parking only once, the customer can visit many different stores under one roof. The idea of the enclosed mall is so popular that larger shopping centers of this type are being built. There is a question of how large these centers can become before they defeat their own purpose. The distances between stores in an extremely large mall and the distance between available parking space and the building itself, become very close to creating conditions where the customer feels that too much walking is involved.

The Strip Center

The strip center has a certain advantage over the mall since usually parking can be closer to the particular stores the customer desires to enter. The important thing in the strip is that all of these stores be air-conditioned and that there be a canopy along the sidewalk so that customers can go from one store to the other without getting out in a rain shower.

Shopping Hours

Another important feature is that the shopping hours of the center be such that they are of the greatest convenience to the people located in the market area.

It is the general trend for shopping centers to be open at night. In order to compensate for the long hours at night, the stores do not open until late in the morning. Experience has proven that these are the most convenient hours for the average shopper, and nearly all shopping centers have come to this arrangement.

In some shopping centers, some stores open on Sunday. This is generally true of the drug store, and in other shopping centers nearly all of the stores are open on Sunday. This is usually caused when the department store decides to adopt this policy, and the other stores are more or less forced to follow suit.

Other conveniences in shopping centers are drive-in establishments wherever possible to have them. The most common types of drive-ins are banks, dry cleaners and laundry pick-ups and liquor stores. Where banks have drive-in windows, they find that a high percentage of their business is transacted in this manner. The same observation is true of dry cleaners and laundries and liquor stores.

The construction of drive-in stores is usually difficult in the center and, in a mall type of center, virtually impossible. However, wherever the architect can fit in a drive-in bank and other drive-in installations that are advantageous, it is of long-term benefit to the center as it draws more shoppers and greater profitability.

ATTRACTIVENESS

In order to try to attract as many customers as possible, any shopping center must present an inviting, clean and beautiful appearance. The first impressions that people get of a shopping center and how it compares in appearance with other competing centers is important. There is something much more pleasant in shopping in attractive surroundings than otherwise.

Buildings

The necessary element of attractiveness is another reason for employing a first class architect. There are many things that can be done to the building at low expense which will make it unique and stand out from surrounding developments and create a favorable picture in the shopper's mind. The design of the roof, the materials used in the walls, the arrangement of doors and windows all contribute to the impression received by the public.

The building should, of course, be modern in construction, as that also creates a favorable image.

Parking Lot

The parking lot must provide an attractive and inviting appearance. The general layout of the lot and the way the parking spaces are marked is very important in this. Here again a good architect is of enormous help.

Other features are the poles on which the lighting for the parking lot is attached. These poles can be of attractive, modern design and will add to the appearance of the center.

Other important considerations are the pylons to support signs identifying the center. The signs themselves should be large, well lighted and easily read from a considerable distance. Attention should also be given that the signs marking entrances and exits be neat and attractive.

Landscaping

Generally speaking the more green areas that a shopping center has in the form of shrubbery or flowers or even just plain grass, the more attractive the center will be. Frequently centers will arrange plantings along the edges of the building, and in the case of strip centers, will have shrubs and flowers in a belt between the sidewalk and the parking area. The area immediately around lamp posts will frequently be landscaped.

Cleanliness

After the shopping center has been built and is in operation, nothing contributes to its attractiveness more than an absolutely clean appearance. The parking lot must be kept free from trash and debris and in most centers, a man works full time on this. Various mechanical sweepers and other devices are obtainable which make it possible for one man to do a great deal of cleaning work.

In the case of the enclosed mall, the public areas must be kept clean and, here again, a full-time man is usually working, if it is a large center.

Nothing can detract from the appearance of a shopping center more than papers, sacks and other debris scattered around the parking lot. In wintertime snow removal becomes an important and sometimes expensive matter. However, the parking lot must be kept usable and snow removed as soon as possible. Another thing that contributes to the appearance of the parking lot is that the lines marking the parking spaces be kept painted well enough to be easily seen. After awhile, the markings tend to be worn by cars driving over them and eventually become so faint that it is difficult to tell just where they are. In this event they should be repainted.

Also the parking lot, especially if it is a blacktopped lot, must be re-covered from time to time. If holes and cracks are allowed to remain in it, it makes a rough surface and certainly is not attractive to customers.

POINTS TO KEEP IN MIND

- *Location.* Actually the first move in developing a shopping center is to find a suitable location that is convenient to shoppers and that has sufficient drawing area with sufficient population and spendable money income to make the shopping center a profitable development. The ease of reaching the center and getting in and out of it is very important.
- *Parking.* The automobile is actually the reason for the development of the shopping center, and its success has largely been due to the ease of parking. The parking lot must be arranged for ease of ingress and egress and convenience of the customer after he enters it.
- *Tenant Drawing Power.* In all types of centers, it is necessary to have at least one or two outstanding tenants who are well known in the community, who operate very modern businesses and do much advertising. These are necessary in order to draw sufficient customers to make the shopping center profitable and also to enable the smaller tenants to get enough customers.
- *Comfort.* People like to shop in comfort and will frequently go to the shopping center that provides this to the best degree. A number of things contribute to comfort in shopping, and all of these should be considered in designing a center.
- *Attractiveness.* The first impressions are very important ones, and the center should be attractive when first seen by a potential shopper. Usually people spend more money in attractive surroundings and in the long run, the attractiveness of the center will be a very important consideration.

Chapter 15

How to Find Good Tenants for Shopping Centers

Since the success of the shopping center depends upon the tenants in it, it is very important that good ones be obtained. The tenants must be good merchandisers in order to serve the customers of the center, and they must have a good financial background. The latter is not only of importance in financing the center, but of importance in its future stability. Any shopping center developer should plan carefully in advance what tenants he wants and how he is going to get them.

WHAT KIND OF TENANTS ARE NEEDED

To start looking for tenants in a logical and intelligent manner, it is wise to stop and make an analysis of what kind of tenants are needed and wanted.

Type of Center

The type of center, whether it be a small neighborhood type or a community center or a very large regional type, will, of course, give a great indication of what kind of tenants you should have in the center. In the case of the small center, perhaps you would only need one or two chain stores and three or four locals; while in the case of the large regional center you might need more than a hundred tenants, starting with a very large department store and ranging from that down to maybe three or four chair barber shops.

After determining the size of the center to be developed, a list of tenants that should be in it is easy to make. In the smaller centers primarily, you need tenants that sell convenient type goods and items for which the average person shops frequently. This is groceries, drugs and the items usually carried by variety stores.

Financing

After you have estimated the cost of the center, both as to land cost and cost of building and developing, it can usually be determined how much financing is required. If a high percentage of financing is needed, then the tenants must be strong ones on whose leases the greatest amount of financing can be obtained. These are, generally speaking, the large nationally known chains that have triple "A" financial ratings. It can easily be discovered through a local mortgage agent, about how much can be borrowed on leases. Due to the recent fluctuations in the availability of mortgage money, it is best to get an up-to-date analysis of this from your mortgage broker, as well as his opinion as to how long the present market for mortgages will exist. It is possible, and has been done at times, that with a sufficient number of triple "A" tenants with long leases, 100 percent of the development cost of the center may be borrowed on a long-term mortgage.

Where a large portion of the total cost of the center must be borrowed on long-term mortgages, the emphasis must, of necessity, be on the tenants who can form sufficient security so that the largest amount of financing can be obtained. In this connection, the amount of financing needed will to a large extent determine the terms of leases. Generally speaking, the longer the lease, the higher proportion of mortgage money that can be borrowed. Where a very large amount is needed, it is best to try to make the leases for at least twenty years or longer.

Where a large amount of financing is not needed, and this would be the case where the developer of the center owns the land outright and has additional cash in a substantial amount to put into its development, a different perspective on tenants can be used. It is generally recognized in the shopping center business that the greatest amount of profit that a developer can make will come from small tenants who can pay him a high rental per square foot and from merchants who can produce a large amount of sales and pay large amounts of sales override. In the cases where large financing is not a problem, the emphasis might be more on smaller successful local tenants who can pay high rental and thereby result, in the long run, in giving the developer a high return and profit on his money.

Needed Income

In any event, undoubtedly the center will be financed in part on mortgage money. The developer should make a careful analysis of the cost of the overall development, the amount of expenses he will have, such as, taxes, insurance, and maintenance on the center, determine how much money it is necessary for him to borrow and, by adding all of these factors together, determine the actual amount of cash that he must have coming in every month.

This consideration will effect to some extent the tenants that he will get in this center. If a comparatively low amount of cash flow is required, he might look for tenants who, while they will not pay so much in fixed rentals, will pay high sales overrides.

In any event, whether the mortgage indebtedness is large or small, there will be a fixed amount of money required every month to cover mortgage servicing and necessary expenses of operation. It is this amount of money that must be covered by guaranteed rental, preferably by rentals received by triple "A" firms who will always pay their rent promptly.

Space

After the type and size of center have been decided, it is possible to determine the amount of floor space that must be leased to tenants. This could enter into, in some instances, the choice of tenants. If it is planned to have two very large department stores, the number of smaller tenants required will, to some extent, be determined by the amount of space left over after renting the two department stores. At any rate, a careful analysis of the space to be filled will give valuable information as to how many tenants are needed and about what size stores they should have.

Outline of Tenant Requirements

After the elements examined above have been determined, it is a good idea for the developer to make an outline of what tenants are needed for the center and about what size space they will be expected to use. The outline he makes could be divided into two sections, one for chain stores and one for locals. The proportion of these would be determined largely by the amount of financing required.

The outline could show such criteria as type of business, space to be filled, minimum rental that can be accepted as well as the minimum terms as to length of lease that are suitable.

After this outline is made it should be checked carefully to see if the basic rents that are covered by this outline are sufficient to pay the necessary monthly cash outgo. It also should be examined carefully to see if there is a sufficient variety of merchandise so the shopper can find most anything he wants in the shopping center.

By developing this outline, the developer knows how he should plan his work. Possibly as the situation develops, he may find that a great many of the things in the outline must be changed, but at least the original outline gives him a plan on which to work and points the direction in which he must go.

Plan of Building

Whatever the plan of building that the architect comes up with, it probably will be changed a number of times before actual construction is started. The actual planned layout of the building will be determined to a large extent by the tenants in it and their requirements. Most large chains have their own building plans and insist on certain dimensions for the stores. For this reason, the final building plans cannot be made until after the major tenants have been obtained.

However by having a building plan, it is possible to get a clear idea as to what tenants are needed, where they can be placed and how much space they will require.

PROMOTIONAL MATERIAL NEEDED

There are many shopping centers being built or planned, and everyone of them is searching for good tenants. For this reason, chain stores are deluged with mail, phone calls, personal calls from shopping center developers and leasing agents. Out of these tremendous number of contacts, the real estate manager for the chain must pick out the 5 or 10 percent that actually are of interest to his company. Therefore when attempting to get chain stores in a shopping center, it is necessary to compete with many other shopping centers. For this reason it is necessary, to have certain promotional material, not only for the purpose of arousing the attention of the real estate manager of the chain store, but also to arouse his interest in your particular proposition.

While local tenants are not so besieged as the chain stores, it is necessary to have material to convince the local merchant that he should have a store in the shopping center. The opening of a store in a shopping center is a very large undertaking for a local merchant and is of immense importance to him. For this reason, it is difficult for him to make up his mind, and good center promotional material is needed.

Feasibility Study

The feasibility study is usually made even before the decision is reached as to whether or not to build a shopping center. The feasibility study is a guide for the developer and enables him to find out whether or not a shopping center is needed in the location he has in mind or whether or not it would be worthwhile and rewarding to build one. The feasibility study is usually made by an independent firm of market research people who study the market area for the proposed shopping center very carefully. Their study will include population studies, income classifications, amount of retail area, competing centers and everything necessary to determine whether or not there is a sufficient amount of spendable money income in the area to justify the building of the shopping center.

This study is usually effected in great detail and divides the amount of retail business available into such catagories as food, drugs, clothing, etc. The value of the study is not only to determine the advisability of actually building the shopping center, but will also point out to a large extent the size of the shopping center that should be built. Since this study furnishes the information as to the potential of the shopping center and gives an indication of the amount of retail business in the various catagories that can be expected, it is exactly the type of information that any prospective tenant would want to have. Some of the chain store real estate managers cover a very wide area, and it is imposible for them to have detailed information about any particular locality. Feasibility

THE OUTER DRIVE STORY

Only seven years ago, the Outer Drive area was four thousand acres of vacant land, in Smithtown, a city of 40,000 people and market center for a predominantly agricultural area. At that time, industry, realizing the many advantages Smithtown had to offer, began to build sizeable factories in the locality and the city started to grow by leaps and bounds. The need for additional homes became apparent.

The Smithtown Development Company, seeing the potential for the four thousand acre tract in the Outer Drive area, purchased it and began a residential subdivision. The location was attractive and easy of access. It grew rapidly. Most of the families brought to Smithtown from other cities by the industrial plants purchased homes there. Today, there are three thousand new homes and nearly 12,000 prosperous people live in the Outer Drive area, plus 60,000 in Smithtown.

From the start, the developers realized that there would sooner or later be a need for a shopping center. They retained sixty acres for the purpose located in the very center of the development and built wide streets leading to it. The location is not only the most convenient one for the twelve thousand people in the immediate area, but also for people residing in other parts of Smithtown and the surrounding countryside. Wide thoroughfares lead to the center from all directions.

This shopping center is now to be developed and will in itself hasten the continued growth of the Outer Drive area, due to the increased attractiveness of the section and the new convenience of the shopping center.

Development of the shopping center is to begin immediately and the target date for the formal opening is to be August 1st of next year. It will be the latest word in comfort and shopping convenience in the form of a closed mall which will be heated and air-conditioned. The parking area will provide a minimum of three square feet of parking space for every square foot of floor area in the mall.

Your earnest attention is invited to what we believe to be one of the outstanding shopping center opportunities in the nation. Smithtown is one of the fastest growing cities in America and the Outer Drive area is its best residential section and its fastest growing one. Write, wire or phone us for maps of Smithtown and its surroundings and a plat of our development.

Prospectus

Exhibit 15-1

studies give them this information and enable them to tell very quickly whether or not their firm should have any interest in the location presented to them. For this reason a number of copies of the feasibility study should be made. They are helpful in obtaining attention on the part of the prospective tenant, and then developing this attention into actual interest.

Plan

A detailed plan of what is proposed in the center should be prepared so that it can be furnished immediately to any tenant that indicates interest. This plan should involve such features as the size of the building, size of the parking lot, the amount of expansion area retained, the type of construction of the building, where it is proposed that the various types of businesses will be located in the center and a time schedule as to when construction is expected to start and when the center is expected to actually open for business.

Along with this outline of the plan for the center, there should be a prospectus written by the developer or leasing agent to point out the most attractive features of the geographical area in which the center is to be built. A sample prospectus used in the development of a shopping center in Lexington, Kentucky is reproduced in Exhibit 15-1.

Locality Maps and Plats

There should be a map prepared showing the exact location of the shopping center and the various streets and roads leading to it. When the developer picks the location, he should pay attention to how the customers would get into and out of the center. This is of importance to the tenants too and the locality map should show this very plainly. Exhibit 15-2 is a sample of one of the maps used in promoting a center in Lexington, Kentucky.

Another item that is an essential is a plat showing how the proposed center is to be built. A sample plat for a shopping center is shown in Exhibit 15-3.

While it is true that the original plat will probably be changed many times and in many different ways, it is necessary to have guidelines to go by, and the plat will show the prospective tenant ap-

Promotional Map

Exhibit 15-2

Courtesy of Pierson-Trapp Company, 1750 Alexandria Drive, Lexington, Ky.

GARDENSIDE PLAZA
1 MILE
2 MILES
To FRANKFORT & VERSAILLES
To Keeneland Race Track, Blue Grass Field Airport, & Frankfort
60
CALUMET LTER
PARKERS MILL RD
STANDISH WAY
COLONIAL
WILLIAMSBURG RD
CROSS KEYS RD
CARLETON ST
SHENANDOAH DR
APPOMATTOX RD
BLUE RIDGE RD
GETTYSBURG RD
CELIA LA
TAZEWELL DR
MASON
WOLF RUN RD
DUNTREATH DR
HEADLEY
PICADOME GOLF COURSE
S ADDISON AV
VERSAILLES RD
CHANTILLY RD
DEANVILLE DR
OXFORD CIR
WESTMINSTER
LONDONDERRY RD
WESTGATE DR
HAMILTON PK
GARRETT AV
WOODFORD DR
GLOVER AV
DELMONT DR
HALLS DR
CISCO RD
TRAFTON ST
Southern RR
FRANKFORT
VILEY
L&N RR
County Infirmary
City Jail
PIKE
LISLE RD
LIGGETT
TEXACO ST
CLYDE ST
WILTON AV
THOMPSON RD
KENTON RD
DEVONSHIRE AV
DUNCAN
BROADWAY
VIRGINIA
Kentucky Trotting Horse Breeders Association FAIR GROUND
BENNETT
PORTER CT
ANGLIANA
ROBERTSON ST
CURRY AV
MANCHESTER
Calvary Cemetery
BUCHANAN
BYARS
PATTERSON
MERINO
PINE
HIGH ST
MAXWELL
SPRING
LIMESTONE
UNIVERSITY
COLFAX ST
PRALL ST
SCOTT
UPPER
LAWRENCE
JERSEY
PLUNKETT
MILL ST
VINE
HARRISON AV
EUCLID
LEXINGTON
MAXWELL
STONE AV
HIGH
BROADWAY
GEORGETOWN
BELT LINE
NEWTOWN PIKE

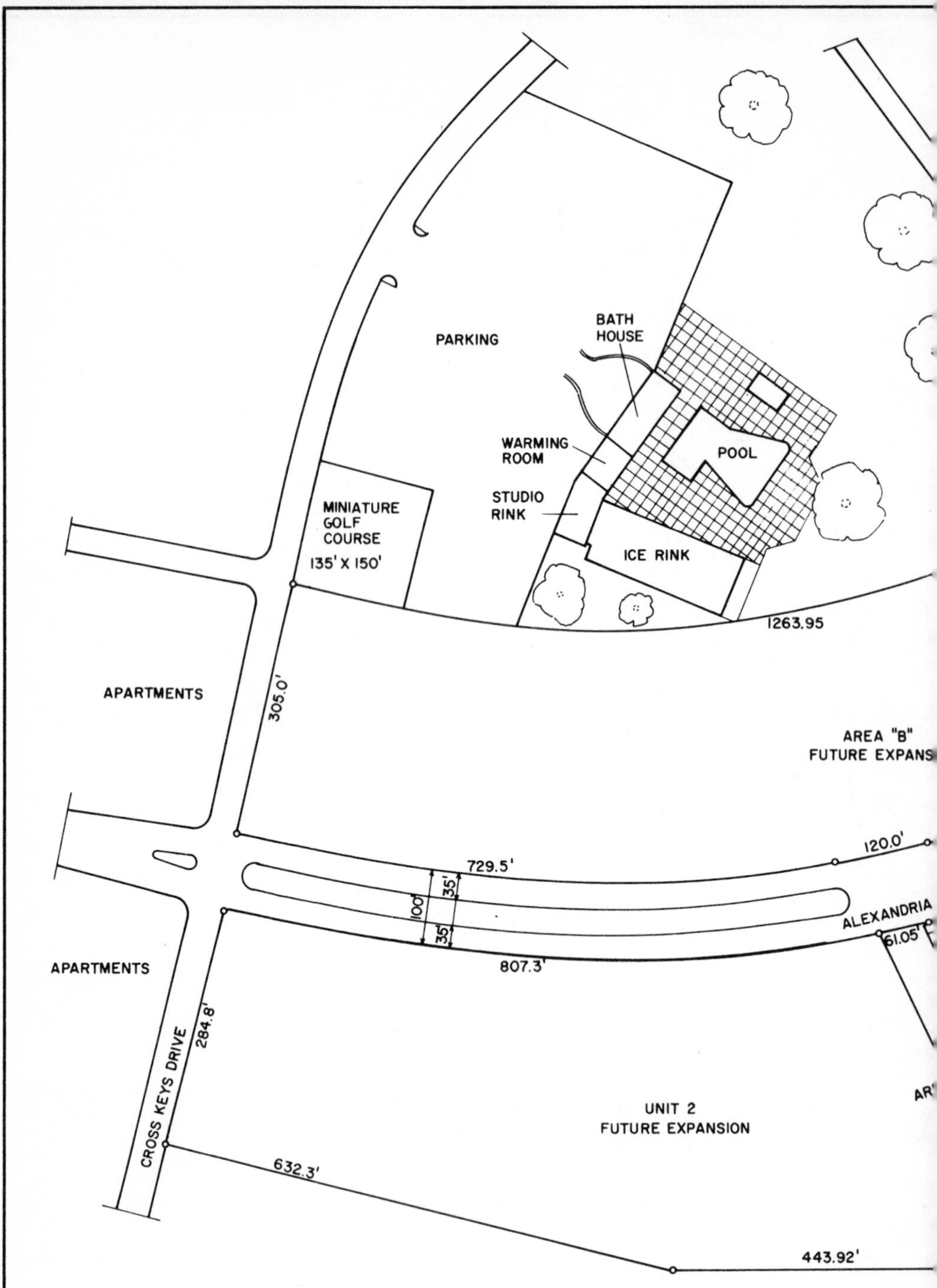

Sample Plat

Exhibit 15-3

Courtesy of Pierson-Trapp Company, 1750 Alexandria Drive, Lexington, Ky.

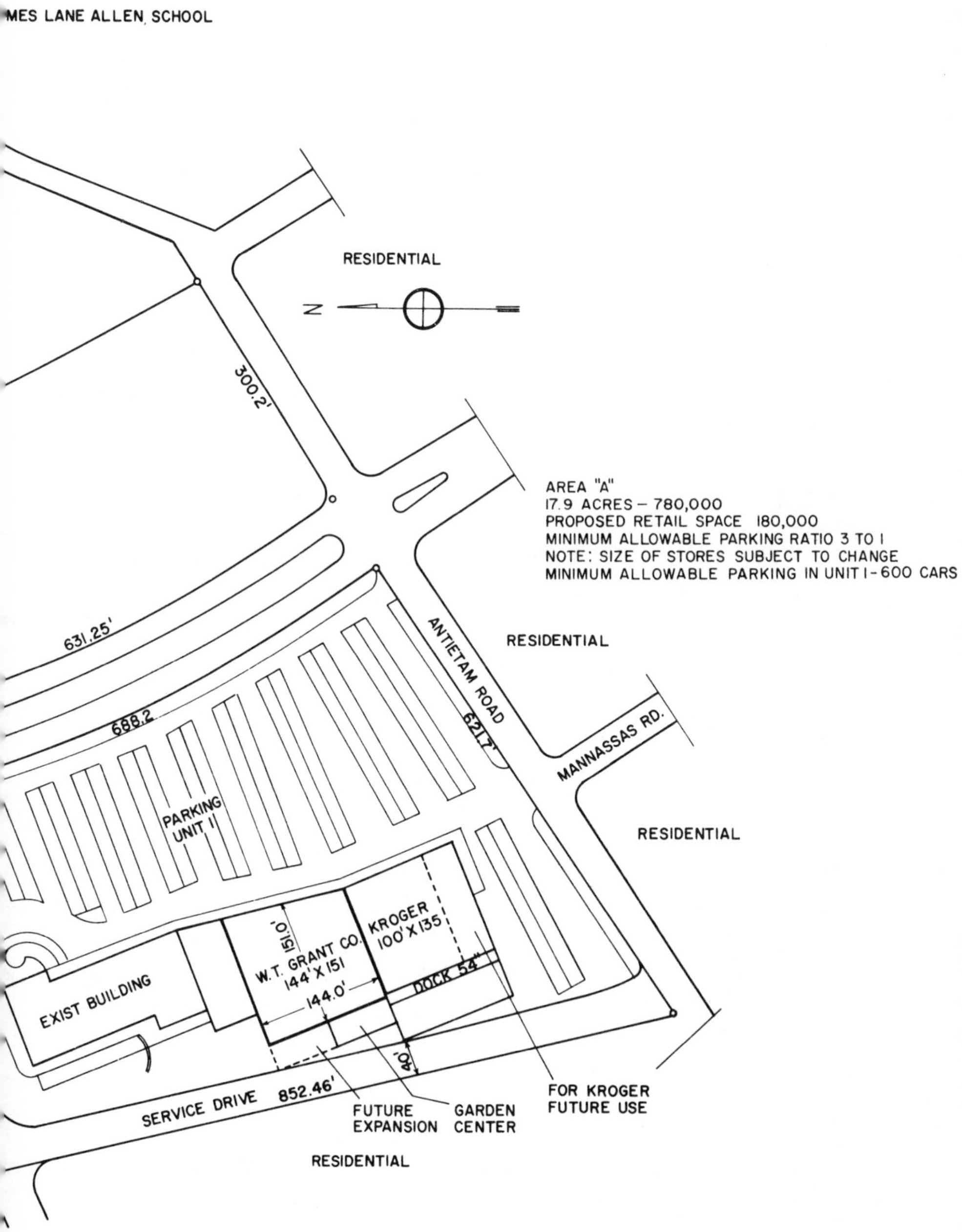

SITE PLAN

GARDENSIDE PLAZA SHOPPING CENTER
PIERSON · TRAPP CO. INC.
LEXINGTON, KENTUCKY

WM. C BRYANT
LEXINGTON, KENTUCKY

proximately what he can expect as to the future development of the shopping center and the actual construction of the shopping center building. In this connection, insofar as the first plat is concerned, most tenants should be told that the plat will be changed and can be changed in order to meet their requirements. This would be especially the case in contacting large department stores or other key tenants, as they will usually have layout plans and the space must be designed to fit these plans.

Illustrations

By the time all this planning has been done, the architect has probably made an artist's rendition of what he expects the center to look like when it is completed. This is a very valuable picture if it is well done, and will emphasize the attractive points that will draw business to the center. Another definite advantage in presenting a shopping center is an aerial photo of it. This shows the amount of residential area built up in the locality and the direction of the various streets. If the area is a growing one, it is an advantage to have two aerial photos if they can be obtained. One of them showing the location a few years previous and another one showing it at the present time. The aerial photos clearly bring out the growth in population of the area.

ADVERTISING

Advertising in the popular media, such as newspapers, magazines, television and radio is probably not of much value except for the large regional type of centers which must have many good tenants that will probably have to be drawn from a rather wide area. In general, where advertising is considered necessary, the media used will vary according to whether or not the tenants being sought are chain store tenants or local ones.

Advertising for Chain Store Tenants

It is important to pick a media that goes to the chain store reading clientele and is read by real estate managers of various chain stores of the country. The *Chain Store Age* magazine has a shopping center edition which is watched by real estate managers of most chain stores. This magazine is full of news and advertisements, and it is well worthwhile to send news of your shopping center to the editor of the magazine along with your advertisement. Plans for your shopping center will then be made a news item, and you will get coverage not only by your paid advertising, but from the news item which will give you good publicity and be widely read by chain store real estate departments.

The important thing in the news item is the size of the center and the location. Many real estate managers can determine by these two factors immediately as to whether or not they have any interest. If they are interested in that locality and in that size center, they will then contact the developer. It is important in the advertisement, besides noting location and size, to have a prominent signature giving the name and address and telephone number of the person who should be contacted for further information about the shopping center. As things progress and the developer obtains a good tenant, the news of such lease having been made can be sent to magazines and local newspapers in the hope that it will be printed as a news item. Nothing succeeds like success, and every time you get a good tenant, you are making it easier to get additional ones. That is the reason why you should keep chain store real estate department managers informed of your progress.

Other media that can be used are, of course, such financial publications as the *Wall Street Journal.* A great many of the chain headquarters are in New York City, and the paper probably most read by them would be the *New York Times;* however, it is doubtful if advertisements in any kind of newspaper are of any particular help in reaching good chain store tenants.

The procedure followed by a great many chain store real estate managers is to visit areas in which they know their company wants stores and conduct a survey of their own. They will try to become familiar with the area and may spend a few days driving around and making inquiries and studying the situation. For this reason it is important that you have an attractive sign on the location for your shopping center. Many chain store tenants are contacted in this manner. When the real estate manager, in familiarizing himself with the area sees the sign, he will probably contact the developer. Information on the sign should give the size of the center, approximately when it is expected to open and the name of the person to be contacted for further information about the center. This sign should be large and easily read from the street or highway in front of it. It should also be tastefully arranged and attractive. The real estate manager may form an instant conclusion as to whether or not your center will be done in an attractive and modern manner by the appearance of your sign.

Other forms of advertising that might be of benefit would be a billboard, especially on the principal traffic artery coming into town from the airport. If properly located and designed, this sign will attract the attention of chain store people when they visit your city. Most of them travel by air, and the most prominent place would be between the airport and the downtown area.

Local Tenants

In advertising for local tenants, the local papers can be useful. Probably the most advantageous would be news items. In a great many instances, the developer does not want his plans to be known locally until he has obtained his principal and strongest tenant. However after this has been obtained, it becomes valuable to let it be known locally what the plans are. The formation of a large shopping center with one or two strong anchor tenants is definitely a newsworthy item and of immense interest to everyone in the city. For this reason you will get news coverage, and by giving information you desire released to the editor of your local paper, you will undoubtedly get a great deal of publicity.

Advertising in the paper need not be extensive, but can be sufficient to at least mention the name of the center, and the name and address and telephone number of the person to be contacted for further information about it.

Here again the sign on the property is certainly one of the very best advertisements for it. Many local people will see this sign and those who do see it will tell other people about it, and the word of mouth advertising that will result will be very considerable.

DIRECT MAIL

Probably the best way to initially contact prospective tenants, especially chain store tenants, is by direct mail. This direct approach must be carefully planned and arranged so that it will actually get the attention of the person to whom addressed. The average real estate manager for the large chains gets a tremendous amount of mail and, due to the time factor, most of it is scanned very briefly. In this connection, an unusual letterhead, one that stands out from the crowd, is very desirable. A little money spent on extra art work for your letterhead, possibly involving the use of color, is very helpful.

Preliminary Letter

The first mailing to the list of prospective tenants should be very short and concise and to the point. It should emphasize three things; the city in which the center is to be built, the size of the center, and the target date for opening. The letter should then briefly suggest to the reader that, if interested, he should write for further and more detailed information including maps, pictures and plats. The name and address to whom he would write for this information should be clearly indicated as well as the telephone number. Exhibit 15-4 is a sample of such a letter which was used successfully.

Date__________

Gentlemen:

Our city, __________, is now the second largest market in our state of __________, and is the fastest growing one. In an area of the city which has an immediate population of over fifty thousand people, with average incomes of over $7,000 per family, we are developing a well-located shopping center.

Our center, when completed, will have 250,000 sq. ft. of building area plus 750,000 or more sq. ft. of parking. We intend to open our center on August first, or thereabouts, of next year. If this sounds like something that would be of interest to you, let us know and we will send you further information, including maps of our city with the location of our center marked, plats of our proposed development and aerial photos showing the homes in the area.

Very truly yours,

Preliminary Letter to Prospective Shopping Center Tenants
Exhibit 15-4

Follow-up Letter

Any answer to the preliminary letter, requesting full information, calls for an immediate response. If the people who answer seem like tenants that would be desirable in the shopping center, they should at this point be sent maps, plats of the proposed development, and possibly a feasibility study. The amount of information sent would probably be determined by the importance of the proposed tenant. If it is one of the department stores that you are especially anxious to acquire, a feasibility study should be included with this follow-up letter.

In addition to the information there should be an invitation to visit your city and see the location in person. It is a good idea to request that, in the event a trip is made to meet with you, that you be advised in advance and also offer to meet the real estate manager at the airport in order to conserve his time while in your locality and to furnish him transportation while he is there.

Along with the other information there should be a write-up of the area, emphasizing the growth that has taken place in the recent past and the future growth anticipated. Usually the Chamber of Commerce can be helpful in supplying pamphlets, some of which can be enclosed with this material.

Generally speaking, it is not necessary to send all of this information to people who do not answer your first letter. This is true in cases except where the prospective tenant is one that you especially want in the center. If it is a key tenant, such as a large department store, that you are especially anxious to have in your center, it might be advisable to go ahead and send the follow-up letter, even though you have not received a reply to your first one.

Telephone Follow-ups

In the event some people to whom you send the follow-up letter with full information do not respond within a reasonable length of time, it is a good idea to follow up by telephone. A direct call to the real estate manager to whom you have sent the full information will usually call it to his mind, and perhaps result in an appointment to come and visit with you. As a logical reason for calling him, you can mention that you are calling him to find out whether or not you supplied him enough information in your follow-up letter to enable him to get some idea as to the extent of his interest.

You can then give him a sales talk about the growth of the area and how fine your development is going to be and suggest that he come and see you as soon as possible. Try to pin him down as to exact date and time of his visit. If you are able to accomplish this, it is a good idea to write him a letter confirming the arrangements, so that they will be firmly fixed in his mind.

Mailing Lists

The most complete list of chain stores at this time is the "Directory of Leading Chain Stores in the United States" published by Chain Store Business Guide, Inc., an affiliate of *Chain Store Age*. It can be obtained through the National Association of Real Estate Boards, Chicago, Illinois or direct from *Chain Store Age*, 2 Park Avenue, New York, N. Y. 10016. This guide classifies chain stores according to the type of business, and in each type of business further classifies them into geographical location of their headquarters. Information such as the number of stores operated by the chain and the states in which they are represented is given, and also the names of the various officers. Usually there will be a vice-president in charge of real estate, and this would be the man to whom you would direct your communications. If you write the main office, you will find that you frequently will be referred to a regional office which serves the immediate locality in which your development is located. This is particularly the case of large chains that are nationwide in scope.

Other mailing lists for chains would be your local telephone directory. You would use the local telephone directory primarily as a source of prospects for your local merchant tenants. However, it will also give you an idea of which chains are already in your area.

In connection with the presentation of your development to chains, it is a good idea to do this far in advance of the target date of your opening. Many of the chains budget their expansion two or three years in advance and, if your development does not get in the works two or three years before the opening of the center, there will usually be a delay in getting chain stores to agree to go in your shopping center.

Logical Chain and Local Prospects

In deciding which particular chain stores to contact in regard to your development, the ones that are already in your state or in neighboring states are the most obvious ones. Usually a chain will expand geographically in relation to its present setup of distribution and warehouses and where new units will be close enough to be supervised from their existing facilities. Sometimes, especially if you contact a chain not already in your particular state, you will find that they will be interested in expansion only if they are able to get several locations at approximately one time. Often they will not enter a new city unless they can open more than one store at about the same time. The reason for this is that advertising in local media such as newspapers and television stations can cover more than one store with the same expenditure. It also makes it easier on their distribution, as trucks coming from their warehouses can carry loads for more than one store. It also makes supervision on the part of the main office personnel more economical, as several stores can be visited on one trip.

Other logical chain store prospects are those that are already in your community but are not located in the area which your development is to serve. This is really a top notch source of prospects, and if the chains in your town or market area are desirable for your development, they may be your best possible prospects. Here again the telephone book is of paramount importance.

In choosing logical locals to approach regarding your center, the telephone book is again of help. Other sources of information might include the Dun and Bradstreet Rating Book which you can probably find at your local bank. There is no point in approaching any local merchants who are not financially strong enough to open a new branch. Observation on the part of the developer in the area will disclose to him which are the best operated local stores. Frequently a glance through the advertising pages of the local paper will also give some good leads as to who is the most aggressive in obtaining business, and therefore most likely to be earning a profit.

PERSONAL CONTACTS

One of the best methods of creating interest in your development is by actual personal contact, by sitting down and talking with the individual concerned.

Method of Approaching Chain Store Companies

In the case of most chain store companies the person with whom you will have your negotiations will be the real estate manager. This is the man that you should see. Usually the first step is to find out where the regional office of the chain is located that serves your area. You can find this out easily through the chain store guide or through calling on one of the local units of the chain store and asking the manager. From the same sources you can find the names of the real estate managers so you will be able to address them properly. Probably the best way to arrange an interview is to call in advance to be sure that the manager will be in his office on the day that you call. Most of these real estate managers do much traveling, and it is always safe to know in advance whether or not they will be available before going to see them.

In further regard to managers of local chain store units, these people are not only a good source of information as to who is the person to see in their regional office, but can also frequently give a good idea as to the amount of interest their firm might have in further expansion in the particular area. They frequently can also furnish information as to the size stores that their company would most likely want.

Logical Contacts for Local Tenants

The owner of the business is, of course, the one with whom you must negotiate, and he is the man on whom you should call. If you have determined that any particular local merchant is financially strong enough and aggressive enough in his conduct of his business to be of interest for your development, the very first thing to do is to make a personal call. In this connection, by calling on him at his place of business, you can get clues as to how desirable he really would be for the development. Usually a good idea as to the success of any business can be obtained very quickly by simply observing how well kept the particular unit is and how customers are treated in the store.

Other sources of leads as to which owners to call on might include your local banker. Frequently the local banker will know which particular firms are interested in expanding and which are not. Other sources of information would probably be your local newspapers which could give you information as to who is doing the most advertising and who is most likely to want to expand with another unit.

By talking to as many local people as possible, you will also run across instances where a particularly good merchant is either losing his lease, or due to some development in the neighborhood and finding it undesirable to stay in his present location, might want to move to a new one. There are very good sources of prospects and should be called on right away as they need new locations.

POINTS TO KEEP IN MIND

- *Kind of tenants needed.* In order to make an overall plan of how to go about getting tenants for your center, it is a good idea to know in advance what it is you are trying to accomplish. You must then plan your efforts along this line in some detail.
- *Promotion material needed.* The amount of promotional material needed will vary a great deal according to the size of the development. For the large regional center you will need much more promotional material than the smaller one, and the minimum consists of feasibility studies, locality maps, plats, pictures and overall plans.
- *Advertising.* Advertising for chain stores would be somewhat different from advertising for local stores, and different publications would be used.
- *Direct by mail.* There are several ways of getting mailing lists for chains that might be interested in your area, and the same applies to smaller local merchants. A direct mail campaign should include both a preliminary and a follow-up letter.
- *Personal contact.* The most effective method of contact is the personal call. The person to see in the chain store office is the real estate manager of the region in which your development is located. As to small local stores, the owner of the business is the one to contact.

It is important that your prospective tenants be contacted far in advance of the target date for opening your center.

Chapter 16

Professional Techniques for Signing Up Shopping Center Leases

The final step in getting leases is obtaining the signatures. Until all of the necessary signatures are obtained, the instrument is completely ineffective. When all the necessary signatures of both parties have been obtained, the lease then becomes a legal and enforceable instrument.

PRELIMINARY STEPS

In the long process, starting from scratch and ending with the signatures actually obtained on the leases, first you must determine what are desirable tenants. There is no point in wasting time on tenants that you do not want anyway. It is necessary to choose tenants that give the center what you want it to have and to select a tenant mix so that no lease conflicts with another. When it is determined whom you want in the center and why, it is time to start the ball rolling.

Selling Job Must Come First

A lease is a complicated instrument and contains many features, of which the most important are the amount of rent to be paid and the length of the lease. In addition to these, there might be from twenty to thirty different provisions of various kinds in the lease.

Some of these provisions are wanted by the prospective tenants, and some of them are wanted by the landlord. As a result, nearly every one of them must be negotiated. How each of the two parties, the landlord and the tenant, make out in these negotiations depends on how well the other party is sold on the shopping center. If a tenant has been properly sold so that he is quite anxious to come into the center, he will be much easier to deal with in the negotiations as to the actual lease instrument. On the other hand, the tenants either consciously or instinctively will try to sell the landlord on the value of having him as a tenant.

The importance of the selling job cannot be overestimated because the profitability of any lease depends to such a large extent on how anxious each party is to do business. From the viewpoint of the landlord or leasing agent, it is a good idea not to sit down and negotiate an actual lease, unless the tenant has been thoroughly sold on the shopping center to the extent where he is anxious to have a store in that center. For this reason it is usually best not to mention any specific terms, until it is certain that the tenant is anxious to do business.

Whether or not the tenant will prove a profitable one for the center will depend to a large measure on the amount of rent he pays and the length of the lease. The more highly he thinks of the location and of the center, the higher the rent he will feel that he can pay, and the more cooperative he will be in agreeing to the various other clauses in the lease.

Quoting Terms

After the selling has been completed, it is then the time to discuss actual terms as to length of lease and amount of rent.

Chain Stores

Before discussing the amount of rent with any chain store, it is a good idea to have clearly in mind what their particular chain usually pays in the way of rent and what length of lease is customary with them. There are various ways in which you can find out about the terms of leases for other units in the particular chain store company. One way to do this is through visiting with owners of other shopping centers in which this chain has stores. Not all shopping center owners will disclose information, but some of them will, and every time you find out about one lease, it helps you to determine just what figures you can plan to quote to that particular chain.

Other excellent sources of knowledge as to terms of any particular chain will come through the mortgage loan company which is doing the financing for the particular shopping center in which you are interested. Usually these mortgage loan companies finance many shopping centers and, in all probability, will have made loans on shopping centers in which this particular chain has stores. Since chain store leases are generally submitted to the mortgage company for their approval, this mortgage loan company will know what rent the chain is paying on other stores. Since the mortgage loan company's interest is in having a mortgage on a successful and profitable center, they will, in most cases, be willing to cooperate in disclosing the information desired.

Once you know what the particular chain is accustomed to paying in the matter of rent and the length of lease that they cutstomarily make, you will have some idea of how to go about quoting terms to them. Much depends on the question of how anxious the chain is to get into your center. It may be that you have other competing prospective chains that are interested in your center, and any of them would like to get in in order to keep the others out. In this case you can usually obtain the highest rental and the longest term of any leases that the particular chain is willing to make. Or, it may be that the particular chain does not have enough units in the market area and is very anxious to have another good one, and in this case you are again in a favorable situation to get the best possible deal.

Generally speaking, the rent that you would quote to the chain would depend on how anxious they are to get into your center, and on the other hand, on how anxious you are to have them. If the shopping center developer has more than one good chain store company that is anxious to come into his center, he is not going to be in any particular hurry to make a lease with any one particular company. Usually the terms of a lease develop into a matter of negotiations, something like playing a game of poker. No chain company that we know of has definite iron bound rules as to the amount of rent they will pay or the length of lease that they will sign. It usually comes down to the matter of who is the best bargainer.

Local Stores

Here again, before quoting a price to a local store, it is a good idea to know what stores are paying in your market area. Usually rentals are figures, as a matter of convenience to the shopping center owner, on the basis of so much per square foot. He knows the cost of his building per square foot and how much rent he has to have in order to cover his expenses and make a profit on the center operation. However, the usual local tenant does not figure rent this way, and it is best not to quote it to the tenant. If the owner wants $2.00 per square foot per year and the store he is talking about is 2,400 square, he would quote $400 a month instead of quoting $2.00 per square foot.

Here again, the actual figures quoted to the local store would depend to a large extent on how anxious the shopping center owner is to have this store in his center and how anxious the local merchant is to be represented in the center. If the selling job has been done properly and the tenant feels that it is very desirable for him to have a store in the center, it will make him easier to deal with.

Since local tenants are not as financially strong as chains, it is much more to the interest of the shopping center developer that the particular local store be able to operate profitably. This factor will be taken into consideration in arriving at the rental terms. The shopping center developer should talk to a number of people in the same line of business as the local prospective tenant so that he will know about how much space the particular tenant would need for a profitable operation and about how much gross margin of profit he makes on his merchandise. Usually it can be determined from these figures about how much rent the prospective tenant can afford to pay and still have a good operation. An important consideration in this regard is in the matter of what other competing tenants you will have in the center. It is a matter of judgment as to how much competition any local tenant can stand from other merchants within the center and how much they will help or hurt the overall situation. It is possible that the size of the center will be such that you would not want to have but one men's clothing store. On the other hand, since women are more inclined to shop around, it might be better to have two or three women's clothing stores. However, it would not be a good idea to have too many, as the business would be split up to such an extent that none of your merchants would make money.

PREPARING LEASES

Leases made with a shopping center tenant are, of necessity, long and complicated. The term of years is usually in excess of ten years, and many leases are for fifteen or twenty or even twenty-five years.

A lot can happen in that length of time, and many questions can arise, and an effort is usually made in shopping center leases to cover as many of these contingencies as possible. For that reason, great care should be exercised in making the lease, and by all means it should be read and approved by the attorney for the shopping center. It will also be necessary for the lease to be approved by the mortgage loan company that is handling the financing on the shopping center.

Leases with Chain Stores

The large national chains have their own lease forms that they like to use. Each chain has its own standardized lease which will run from two to thirty pages. Since a lease which a chain likes to use is prepared by the legal department of that particular company, its provisions are usually entirely in favor of the tenant and will present many advantages to the chain store company. For this reason, the lease must be read very carefully, not only by the shopping center developer, but by his attorney.

Since the various chain store companies are interested in expanding and in keeping up with the growing population and spendable money income, they do want to make completed leases on good locations. For this reason, they usually keep most of the provisions in these leases flexible and, by negotiation between the chain store and the shopping center developer, there can be many changes made to make the lease more fair to each party.

It is of some advantage to the shopping center developer to get a copy of the lease form used by the particular chain with which he is negotiating. Sometimes this is rather difficult to do as the chain store real estate manager is frequently instructed by his company not to give any of these lease forms to anybody until everything has been agreed upon and the lease has been written in final form by the chain store attorney. When this lease is finally presented to the shopping center owner, he can then examine it very carefully and in discussion with the chain's real estate manager settle any differences of opinion there may be as to the terms, provisions and wording of the lease.

Leases with Local Tenants

It is usually necessary for the shopping center developer to have the leases prepared for the local and smaller tenants. For this purpose, he will find it convenient to have his attorney prepare a standardized lease form that he will try to use with all of the other smaller tenants. In this way he can have approximately the same provisions for everyone. Usually these local tenants, after they are in the center, get to know each other and will invariably compare the rentals and other terms of the leases each one has signed. If the leases are as near the same as possible, a certain amount of ill will and argument can be avoided.

This lease form which the developer will use should cover as many contingencies as possible, and at the same time the lease should be as short as possible. Many local tenants are immediately suspicious of a long legal document and become fearful that they will commit themselves to something they do not understand. For that reason, it is definitely of advantage to have a lease form that covers the important things, but is as short as possible. The developer should know which provisions of the lease he will have to insist on and know in advance the things he cannot change. As to the other provisions of the lease which are flexible, he should have an idea as to just how far he can go in making changes to conform to the wishes of the prospective tenant.

After the lease has been prepared, a copy should be sent to the tenant so that he can examine it carefully and, if he desires, submit the lease to his attorney and have it checked by him.

It is important that the prospective tenant understand the lease in its entirety. Sometimes a meeting with the developer, the developer's attorney, the tenant and the tenant's attorney to go over the lease paragraph by paragraph is wise. It would not do for something to occur bringing into effect a provision of the lease and have the tenant claim that he did not know about this provision or did not understand it. It always makes for good relations between the landlord and tenant to have everything well understood by both parties before the lease is actually signed. Such a meeting can be easily arranged, and it is best to have it at the developer's office as, we have found from experience, it is usually easier to get complete agreement if the meeting is held in the developer's office rather than at the office of one of the attorneys or of the tenant.

NEGOTIATING DIFFERENCES BETWEEN LANDLORD AND TENANT

In any instrument as long and complicated as a shopping center lease, there are certain to be differences of opinion between the two parties concerned. Before the lease can be finally signed and put into effect, these differences must be resolved. Usually a meeting is held in which the various provisions of the lease are gone over one at a time and frequently changed to effect a compromise between the landlord and the tenant.

Inflexible Provisions

Each party to the contract will have certain considerations in mind on which he does not feel there can be any compromise. On the landlord's part, it might be the length of lease. The minimum term of any lease into which the landlord can enter might be dictated by the mortgage loan company, and the same applies to minimum terms. If the mortgage loan company has insisted that the landlord sign no leases shorter than a certain given number of years with no rental lower than a certain figure, these things are inflexible from the landlord's standpoint. If it is determined that the tenant is not willing to meet these criteria, there is no choice except to abandon the tenant and seek another one.

The tenant will sometimes have inflexible conditions too. These may concern percentage of sales clauses or length of lease. If the landlord is unwilling to agree to the things which the tenant feels are absolutely essential, usually the lease negotiations are quickly terminated.

Flexible Provisions

Fortunately by far most of the clauses and conditions in the lease are flexible and where there is a disagreement, some compromise can be worked out. In negotiations between the tenant and the landlord, much depends on how firmly each one is sold on the other. If the tenant is anxious to get into the center and has been sold on the idea that it is extremely advantageous to him to do so, he will be much easier to deal with in the final drawing of the lease. The same observation applies to the landlord. If the tenant is a large department store and the only one that the landlord feels he can get in the center, the department store company can almost draw its own terms, since the landlord is more or less forced to go along with it if he is going to have a complete center. However, if both sides are reasonable people, as is usually the case, some compromise that is fair to both parties can be worked out.

A sample of one clause which can usually be compromised is the tax escalation clause. This clause in the lease calls for an increase in rent if the local property taxes are increased. From the landlord's standpoint, he would like to have the rent increased sufficiently to cover any increase in property taxes and, of course, the tenant would prefer not to have the clause. If the tenant objects to this clause and the landlord feels it should be in there, a compromise is frequently reached on the basis of the landlord agreeing to absorb part, possibly half, of any property tax increases and the tenant agreeing to absorb the other half by proportionate increase in rental. Another way that this difference is frequently compromised is by the landlord agreeing to absorb any increase in property taxes for a matter of two or three years, and then after that if the taxes are further increased again, the tenant will bear them in the form of increased rental.

Other clauses that frequently lead to differences between two parties include the percentage of sales clause. This is a necessary provision for the landlord to have and is usually inflexible. However, the amount of the percent of sales which will be put in the lease can frequently be compromised. Actually, in most businesses, there is a fairly well standardized percentage which is customary. The percentage varies immensely from one kind of business to another. The supermarket with its large volume and extremely low margin of profit may only pay 1 percent to 1¼ percent of sales. This is all the store can afford to pay and all the landlord usually expects. Where there is a percentage fairly well recognized throughout the industry, usually there is no problem in arriving at the percentage amount. However, frequently there are some businesses where percentages, by custom, vary a great deal. In this case, it is necessary for the landlord and tenant to arrive at a mutually attractive figure. In the case of a ladies' clothing store, the landlord may think that he should have a 6 percent of sales clause, and the tenant may think he should only have 4 percent. Frequently these differences can be compromised by making a sliding scale of rentals. For instance, in this case it might finally be agreed that as soon as the tenant sales reach the point where 6 percent of the sales equals the fixed amount of rent, he will pay 5 percent of sales on any excess over that amount in addition to the regular guaranteed minimum rate. Sometimes the rental percentage can go down as volume increases, to make a greater incentive on the part of the tenant to increase sales and to spend more money in advertising, which not only benefits the tenant and the shopping center, but other tenants in the center.

There are countless examples of clauses in leases in which there can be differences of opinion and which can be usually worked out. From the landlord's point of view he must be specially careful of any loopholes on the tenant's part whereby the tenant can get out of the lease. Usually this part of the lease is checked very carefully by the mortgage loan company's attorney, and whatever he insists on in this regard, must be done.

On the tenant's part he must be very careful as to what restrictions are put on his business. In order to protect other tenants in the center, the landlord will usually try to avoid any overlap in types of merchandise sold so as to eliminate competition between stores in the center as much as possible. Sometimes these restrictions take the form of type of merchandise and sometimes the price ranges of merchandise. In any event, the tenant should very carefully check the restrictions to be sure that they do not affect his business too much.

FINAL LEASE PREPARATION

Since the lease will be a legally binding document for a long period of time, great care must be exercised in making the final lease which is actually signed by all parties. It should be legible, on a good grade of paper, and very carefully typed and read so that there will be no mistakes, however slight. Sometimes a minor mistake pertaining to one word, or even punctuation marks, can change the meaning of the lease, especially if read several years after it has been completed and signed.

Chain Store Lease Preparation

Since the chain stores usually have their own standardized lease forms which they insist on using, the final lease will undoubtedly be prepared by the chain store legal department. When this lease is received by the landlord, he must scrutinize it carefully and have it checked by his own attorney to be sure that everything is in accordance with the agreements reached and that the instrument is worded properly and conforms to local law.

The chain store in sending the lease should send at least three copies, so that two can be signed and returned to the store for their signature. The third copy can be retained by the landlord's office and compared with the completed and signed lease as returned by the chain store company. Quite frequently the chain store company will also furnish a shorter form lease which does not cover all the information in the actual lease itself but which can be recorded in the local clerk's office and made a matter of public record there. This is usually done and omits the actual amount of the rental, but is notice to the public that certain premises have been leased for a number of years by the chain store company.

Before signing the lease, it is usually necessary to have it read carefully by the mortgage loan attorney. Even if the mortgage loan company does not always insist on this, it is a good idea to get both the approval of the mortgage loan company and the opinion of the mortgage loan company's attorney. These attorneys have had a great deal of experience in reading and criticizing leases and sometimes can be very valuable in pointing out things that should be changed in the leases. The mortgage loan company is very sensitive to any possible loopholes by which the tenant might possibly at some future time avoid paying the agreed upon rental. For that reason, the mortgage loan attorney will sometimes insist on changes in the lease, which are almost always to the benefit of the landlord.

Local Stores

Usually it is up to the landlord to prepare the final lease for the local merchant to sign. There should be at least three copies made, one for the landlord, one for the tenant and one to be kept by the landlord's attorney. These leases probably will not be quite as complicated as the chain store lease, but they will be according to the standardized form arranged by the landlord's attorney and will therefore cover a considerable period of time and many possible contingencies. Here again, it is necessary to be very careful in typing a final lease so that there are no errors in it and no possible room for future disagreements between the parties.

Sometimes it is necessary to send these leases to the mortgage loan company before signature and sometimes not. Undoubtedly the landlord, when he makes his standardized lease for local tenants, should file a copy of it with the mortgage loan company to be sure that it meets with their approval. If the standardized lease is not changed in any respect in making any particular contract, it is usually not necessary to send this to a mortgage loan company since they have already approved of the lease form.

However, frequently there are changes made by negotiation between the parties, and the lease in its final form will frequently be different from the standardized form. In this case, it is a good idea to have this sent to the mortgage loan company and have it approved by them, before actually being signed by either the tenant or landlord.

GETTING LEASES SIGNED AND PROCEDURES IN DOING SO

The final step in any lease is, of course, the signatures of both parties. Actually the lease is never completed until signed by everyone necessary, at which time it becomes a legal binding document on both the landlord and the tenant.

Who Signs

A lease is not a legally binding contract until the properly authorized signature has been obtained. In the case of a corporation, who is authorized to sign the corporate name and bind the corporation with such signature? Usually there is an officer of the corporation, either a president or a vice-president, who is designated by the corporation as the individual with the power to sign leases. Generally speaking, any officer of the corporation can bind the corporation by signing the lease. In some cases, an attest by the developer's attorney can advise him as to whether this is necessary.

Regarding leases to be signed by individuals or a partnership, in an individual proprietorship, the owner of the business is, of course, the only one that can sign a completed lease. In the event of a partnership, the partnership name should be signed by one of the partners. Any partner can usually bind the partnership, but it is a good idea to have more than one partner sign the lease. It is important to be sure that the tenant is bound by the signature of the person who is authorized to do so.

Franchise Stores and Guarantors

A great many stores throughout the nation are owned and operated by individuals under the name of a large company that grants them a franchise in their area. The Ben Franklin Store is an outstanding example of this. Each store is owned by an individual and operated by him, but the merchandise is obtained from the large national company and operates under the trade name of such large company. Usually they have exclusive franchise rights in a certain area.

In order to make their leases financially strong enough to compete with other chains and to enable the owner of the individual store to obtain the same consideration as given the large national chain, the parent company will frequently cosign the lease. This means that they will guarantee payment of the rental, and makes the lease as strong as the credit of the guaranteeing corporation. In many cases, this is the only way in which the individual lease can be made as strong as the chain store lease for the purpose of obtaining mortgage loan money. Wherever it is possible to get a franchise company to cosign along with the individual owner, it is definitely to the advantage of the shopping center developer to do so. Care must be exercised in obtaining the signature of the guaranteeing company, that it be signed by the proper executive who has the power to commit the corporation.

In the case of individuals, sometimes guarantors can be obtained from other individuals. Usually this is the case where the guarantor is a member of the same family as the tenant. Frequently an ambitious young man will want to start a new store, but his credit is not established, and the landlord is reluctant to take a lease based solely on the signature of the young individual. In many cases the individual tenant's father will cosign the lease. This would be of value where the father's credit has been established and where he has a substantial financial statement. On all individual leases, the shopping center developer should have the prospective tenant file a financial statement with him. Usually this financial statement is required by the mortgage loan company anyway. If the individual does not disclose considerable financial strength, the idea of having a guarantor cosign the lease with him should be fully explored.

FINAL STEPS IN GETTING SIGNATURES

If all of the preliminary work has been well done, usually the final steps of obtaining the signature are very simple.

Chain Stores

After the lease with a chain store has been received in its final form from the legal department of the chain and checked by the mortgage loan company and by the developer's attorney, the developer then can sign the lease in duplicate and send both copies to the proper office of the chain. Usually the actual signature of the chain is the last thing obtained. Some chains are very prompt about signing leases, and the lease will be returned signed by the proper official a week or two after sending it. Some others take a longer time, especially the very large chains where it is sometimes necessary to send the lease a long way for the proper signatures. Anyway, close attention should be paid to the matter and followed up to see that the lease is returned within a reasonable length of time.

Leases with Individuals or Partnerships

My experience has indicated that it is best to have the individual or the partners come to the office of the developer and sign the lease in the developer's office; the developer can sign the lease at the same time and thus make a completed instrument out of it. Usually in taking a lease to an individual's place of business for his signature, there are many interruptions and confusion, and it takes a more extra time than is necessary in the developer's office. There is a natural reluctance on the part of many people to actually and finally commit themselves to a long-term agreement calling for the payment of a substantial sum of money, and any interruption that may occur at the individual's place of business can be used as an excuse to put off the final commitment. Having the parties all gathered in the developer's office prevents this. In the event that a notary public is required to attest the signatures, be sure to have one on hand so that there will not be any delay in finding one.

POINTS TO KEEP IN MIND

- The selling job should be carefully done. If the prospective tenant is properly sold on the center, the other things necessary are made much easier.
- *Preparing leases.* Leases must be prepared properly and with

meticulous care, as they are very complicated instruments that cover the passage of a long period of time.

- *Adjusting differences.* In any instrument that covers a long period of time with as many different provisions as shopping center leases have, there are bound to be many cases where the landlord and tenant fail to immediately agree. Care must be exercised to be sure that all of these differences are resolved. They are usually worked out by some means of compromise.
- *Final Lease Preparation.* The final lease ready for signature should be free of errors and should cover the exact agreement between the parties. It should be carefully checked by the developer's attorney and also by the legal department of the mortgage loan company that is handling the financing for the shopping center.
- *Getting leases signed.* The lease does not become a final legal binding document until signed by all parties. Be sure that the individual who has the power to bind the tenant and the individual who has the power to bind the landlord both sign the instrument. If all of the preliminary steps have been properly completed, there should be no problem in getting the final signatures. Be sure to get a guarantor's signature also if that seems desirable in the circumstances.

Chapter 17

How to Write the Most Lucrative Shopping Center Leases

Shopping center leases are long and complex with many provisions which must be understood by both parties. The leases must be prepared in a manner to make the various provisions as easily understood as possible, and should be checked by attorneys for both the landlord and the tenant to be sure that everything is properly expressed and in legal terminology.

BASIC LEASE PROVISIONS

While there may be thirty or forty or more clauses in the lease, there are certain things that are of paramount importance that must be in all leases.

Amount of Rent

This is probably the most important provision of the lease and usually the one on which there is the greatest difficulty in obtaining agreement of both parties. The two figures that are important are the fixed monthly rental and the sales override. The fixed basic rental is necessary from the landlord's viewpoint, as it is required by the mortgage loan company since he must have a definite fixed income in order to cover the mortgage payments, taxes and other expenses of operation of the center.

The sales percentage clause, sometimes referred to as sales override, is, in the long run, just as important to the landlord as the basic fixed rental. In the event of continuing inflation, the fixed dollar rental becomes of less value as the dollar declines. However, due to the increase in price of most retail merchandise, the sales volume of the tenant will tend to increase and bring into effect the percentage clause. Usually the percentage clause calls for a percentage of sales to be paid as rent if the amount of rent, figured in this manner, exceeds the basic minimum. As an example of this, a lease calling for a basic rental of $1,000 so long as the tenant's sales volume does not exceed $20,000 per month, but when his sales volume reaches the point where it exceeds $20,000 per month, then the 5 percent sales clause would go into effect and would determine the amount of rental.

Sometimes in these sales percentage clauses, the tenant will want certain things excluded. It is generally customary that transfers of merchandise from one store of the company to another be excluded and not be counted as sales. It is also rather usual in drug store leases to exempt the sales of cigarettes and tobacco products from the gross sales for the purpose of calculating the rent, because the margin of profit on these items is extremely small.

Another provision that is usually in the lease in connection with sales percentage is the right on the landlord's part to examine the tenant's books anytime he wishes to verify the fact that proper rental is being paid.

Length of Term

Another basic provision of the lease is the length of time that the lease covers. Seldom in shopping center leases is the term less than five years, and generally it is much longer than this. From the landlord's point of view, the length of lease is especially important in financing a center. It is possible to obtain greater financing on long-term leases, and generally speaking the longer the lease, the more financing that can be obtained. Sometimes the tenant will also like as long a lease as possible, especially if he is well sold on the location and if he knows that other locations in the area might be difficult to obtain in later years. Sometimes, shopping center leases will run as long as twenty to twenty-five years, or in cases where a shop is especially designed for a particular type of customer, such as a theatre for instance, the lease might run even longer.

Options to Renew

An option to renew usually gives the tenant the choice of continuing the lease beyond the primary term if he should so desire. The option is not too desirable from the viewpoint of the landlord, since it does not bind the tenant, but does bind him. For this reason it is generally considered advisable never to allow the options of the lease to exceed in number of years, the primary terms of the lease. If the primary term of the lease is fifteen years, the tenant should never be allowed more than three five year options to renew.

USUAL PROVISIONS IN SHOPPING CENTER LEASES

Certain provisions are found in virtually all shopping center leases and are in fact necessary with all tenants.

Starting Dates

If the space rented is already constructed and ready for occupancy, the starting date would usually be determined by the time required for the tenant to move in. However, most shopping center leases will be completed before the premises leased are actually finished or, in many cases, before construction is even started. For this reason, the establishment of a starting date that is satisfactory to both parties presents certain difficulties. The shopping center developer will usually know how long it takes to complete a store room, but he must be very careful to allow for possible delays which could occur due to bad weather conditions or strikes. Generally this is covered by having a starting date arranged when the developer thinks he can have the storeroom ready, but with a provision in the lease giving him an extra ninety to one hundred twenty days in the event of construction delays.

When Rent Is Payable

Usually the fixed amount of rental is paid on a monthly basis, generally on the first day of each month, monthly in advance. The percentage clause is generally figured on a year's sales, and for that reason cannot be paid until the end of a fiscal or calendar year. The payment is usually due from thirty to sixty days after the end of the year in order to give the tenant time to bring his books up to date. At that time, the percentage rent for the year is calculated, and if it comes to more than the amount that has been paid as basic fixed dollar rental, the difference then becomes due and payable. This provision in the lease will usually carry a clause describing what occurs in the event the tenant fails to pay his rent. Usually this clause will state that, in the event the tenant becomes overdue in his rental payments by as much as thirty days, the landlord can cancel the lease at his option.

What Landlord Furnishes

This clause will usually cover the size of the storeroom to be furnished to the tenant by the landlord and the actual dimensions of the space given. If there are special items pertaining to the store front or interior construction that are agreed upon, all of these should be set out in the lease, so that there will be no disagreement when the storeroom is completed and turned over to the tenant.

Seldom does the landlord furnish any equipment such as store shelving or display cases, etc. It is usually mentioned in the lease that all of these are furnished by the tenant.

Maintenance of Premises Leased

Generally speaking, most shopping center leases call for maintenance of the outside of the building by the landlord and maintenance of the inside of the building by the tenant. In regard to the parking lot, this is almost always the responsibility of the landlord, but sometimes the responsibility for maintenance is turned over to a merchants' association. Most of the time in these leases, there will be contributions made by the tenants for maintenance of the parking lot. The amount of contribution by the tenant is set out in the lease and is based on the amount of square footage occupied by that particular tenant. This can be 5 cents per year per square foot or 10 cents per square foot, depending on the estimated cost of maintaining the parking lot. Another clause in this provision will pertain to the heating and air conditioning equipment. Usually the tenant will be responsible for normal maintenance of this equipment, and the landlord will be responsible in case of a total breakdown calling for replacement of the original equipment.

Legal Description of Shopping Center

Nearly all tenants insist that a legal description of the shopping center be made as part of the lease, either in the lease itself or, as is more usual, by an amendment or schedule attached to the principal lease. Also in the lease should be specified very definitely the exact location of the premises rented. This is usually done by attaching to the lease a plat of the shopping center, with the area to be occupied by the tenant plainly outlined on it.

Interruption of Occupancy

The shopping center lease must cover the contingency of what happens, in the event of some disaster which interrupts the tenant's occupancy of the area that he has rented. This is usually a fire or civil disturbance, or something of that nature. If the premises are rendered unfit for occupancy by the tenant, there should be a clause pertaining to the rental. During the time that the storeroom cannot be used, there should be no rental paid. The landlord should be given an opportunity to put the premises back in condition suitable for occupancy, and usually there is a time limit as to how long he is allowed in which to do this. In the event the premises are not suitable for occupancy beyond a definite stated time in the lease, the lease will become null and void and automatically cancelled.

SPECIAL PROVISIONS OF SHOPPING CENTER LEASES

There are many things that usually appear in a shopping center lease that are designed especially for use in shopping centers in an attempt to overcome certain problems that may arise in the future.

Tax Escalator Clause

After a shopping center has been built and is in business, the value of the property tends to increase. The tax assessors take quick advantage of this by increasing the assessment and thereby increasing property taxes in some to the extent that these taxes are tripled or quadrupled. Without a tax escalation clause, the landlord would find it necessary to bear this considerable increase in expenses without a corresponding increase in income. In order to avoid this contingency, a clause is put in the lease whereby, in the event the property taxes are increased, the increase shall be borne by the tenant. Naturally it is to the tenant's interest to leave this out if he can. In negotiating this matter, frequently a compromise is reached by having the tenant and the landlord each bear half of the increase. Another method of compromising this matter is for the landlord to bear any increases for a period of two or three years after the start of the lease, and for the tenant to bear any further increases after that date. The increased expense due to the taxes is usually added to the rental figure, and the annual increase divided by twelve is added to each month's rent.

Maintenance of Common Area

This means lighting the parking lot, keeping it clean, removing snow, keeping the parking space adequately defined by white lines and keeping up any shrubbery or trees that there may be in the outside areas. It is necessary to have one person responsible for doing this and in almost all cases, it becomes the duty of the landlord. This expense must be covered in the basic rentals, or by an additional rent usually referred to as parking lot maintenance which is assessed to the various tenants on the ratio of their floor area to the total area of the center.

Merchants' Association

It is considered advantageous to have a merchants' association to which the various tenants in the shopping center belong. This association can have various centerwide promotions which improve business for everyone in the shopping center. Some shopping center developers make the membership in the merchants' association voluntary, but most of the best ones make membership a requirement, and is so stated in the lease. The dues to the merchants' association are paid on a basis proportionate to the size of the stores. This is, of course, based on a square foot area and makes the larger stores pay proportionately more than the smaller ones. Frequently in the lease it is set forth that the dues to the merchants' association will not exceed a certain amount per square foot. This is so that no tenant will be reluctant to have this clause in his lease for fear that the dues would be excessive.

It is generally considered better to have the membership a definite obligation because, when the membership in the association is left on a voluntary basis up to the merchant, there are always a few that will not join the association in order to avoid paying dues. These same merchants, however, benefit from the promotion activities of the association without paying their proportionate part.

Guarantee of Major Equipment

It is customary for the tenant to be responsible for day-to-day maintenance of air conditioning and heating and other mechanical equipment and for minor repairs on same, but failure of these appliances due to defect or ordinary wear and tear which results in their replacement becomes an obligation of the landlord. This is usually covered by a separate provision in the lease and is occasionally spelled out in some detail as to what guarantee is placed on the equipment by the landlord. Since frequently this equipment is also covered by a guarantee of the manufacturer, that is also mentioned in this clause.

Lighting of Store Windows

A major portion of the business in shopping centers is done in the evening after dark. It is therefore essential that the center be well lighted. Lighted store windows are a part of the necessary illumination. The appearance of the center and the lighting continuity can be greatly disturbed by a few stores that decide not to open in the evening and do not turn on their window lights. For this reason there is usually a provision in the lease requiring the tenant to have his windows lighted during certain hours of the evening.

Advance Rental

Frequently with small local tenants, there is difficulty in getting sufficient financial information so that the developer of the center will be assured of receiving his rental payment according to the lease. In order to protect the developer in a case like this, frequently a clause is inserted in the lease calling for the payment of a year's rental in advance. Usually this year that is paid in advance is the last year of the lease. In addition to the final year of the lease in advance, the tenant, of course, makes his monthly payments as they arrive. The effect of this is that if the tenant fails to pay his rent or discontinues business, the landlord has several months, possibly up to twelve, of advance rental to replace the income while he is seeking another tenant.

Tenant Installed Equipment

Sometimes in negotiating lease terms, a lower building cost can be obtained by the developer and a lower rental by the tenant installing the air conditioning and heating equipment at his own expense, in which case he would, of course, be the owner of this equipment. This is sometimes done especially with appliance dealers, where the tenant has his own equipment anyway or is a dealer for it and feels that he would like to use certain equipment in which he deals and for which he can usually get an attractive price from the manufacturer.

In this case, of course, the tenant is not only liable for the day-to-day maintenance, but for the replacement of equipment too, since it belongs to him and not to the landlord. In the event the tenant does put in his own mechanical equipment, the clause pertaining to landlord's liability for same would be omitted from the lease.

Special Fronts and Decorations

Frequently a tenant will feel that he should have a special store front which fits his business better than the one used in other stores in the center. If this different type of store front is compatible and fits in well with the rest of the center, the landlord will often fix it as the tenant wishes. Usually this makes an extra building cost and, of course, affects the rent. In any event, since the lease would be made, signed and completed before the actual work was done, it must be set out in a special provision just what type of front is to be put in. Also in this section of the lease should be set out anything else that is unusual that the landlord agrees to do for the tenant. Sometimes this concerns partitions inside the store, special loading provisions in the rear or special decorations. Sometimes as a rider to the lease, actual plans are attached to show exactly what the understanding between the two parties is about these special things.

Restrictive Clauses

Almost every shopping center lease will have certain restrictive clauses. The tenant will try to get as much protection from competition within the center as possible and will try to get restrictions against competing stores. The landlord, on the other hand, will want to protect tenants that he is already committed to and will try to put certain restrictions on the tenant. Usually as a result of negotiations between the parties, certain restrictions on both sides are agreed upon.

Usually in a small center, the supermarket will receive an exclusive in the center for grocery items. If expansion of the center is planned later, this restrictive clause might apply only to the first phase of the center or to a minimum number of square feet of building area. After this first phase is completed, or after the required square footage of building area is completed, the developer can then proceed to negotiate with a second supermarket.

In this connection, the developer must be very careful to keep himself familiar with all of his restrictive clauses in his leases so that he will not make any leases that will conflict with previous ones. For an example, suppose a developer has made a lease with a liquor store giving him the exclusive right to sell liquor in the shopping center, and then he starts negotiating with a drug store concern. It will be necessary for him to put a clause in the drug store lease to the effect that the drug store could not carry liquor, as this would be required to protect the developer from the commitment he has already made with the liquor store. In a large center where there are many stores, the developer must be very careful to keep in mind all of the various restrictions in the various leases or otherwise he might find himself with cancelled leases or damage law suits.

Ownership of Tenant Changes Hands

After a center, especially a large one, has been in business for any length of time, occasions will arise where a particular tenant will sell out to someone else. In the event of local tenants, this may be due to the death or disability of the owner or, in the case of chain stores, there might be a change in ownership of the entire company, or the chain may decide to sell certain stores in certain areas.

In any event, there should be a clause in the lease about this possibility usually to the effect that the tenant cannot escape the responsibility of rental payments, even though he sells to someone else. It should also be stated that any new owner of the business will be bound by all of the clauses of the lease. It is usually stated in this section that the tenant cannot rent his store to someone else without the consent of the shopping center owner. This is an obvious protection for the shopping center developer who wants the center to always have acceptable and good tenants.

Rental Guaranteed by Others

Quite frequently payment of the rental is guaranteed not only by the tenant signing the lease, but by a cosigner also. There should be a special provision in the lease calling for this if that is the case. Frequently a subsidiary company will have its lease cosigned by the stronger parent company. Also frequently in the case of franchises, the national financially strong company will cosign the lease with the individual franchise owners.

Insurance Coverage

In nearly all cases the landlord is responsible for carrying extended coverage insurance on the buildings and also liability insurance on the parking lot. The tenants are required to carry their own insurance on their fixtures and merchandise. Generally it is specified in the lease that the tenant is required to carry liability insurance for accidents that may occur in his store or on the sidewalk immediately in front of his store. It is also usually mentioned in this clause of the lease that this policy carried by the tenant must also name the landlord as protected under the terms of the policy. Usually the minimum amount of liability coverage that is required will also be stated.

Attached Plats

In order that there will be no uncertainty whatever as to the premises leased, a plat of the leased store is usually attached as a separate schedule to the lease. The chains practically all require plats of the entire shopping center to show how much area is covered by the restrictions in the lease. This is usually on a separate sheet and attached to the rest of the lease.

Signs on Store Fronts

In order for the center to have a uniform appearance, there is usually a clause in the lease which sets out the kind of signs which each tenant is allowed to have. Many shopping centers only allow them to have signs that are flat against the front of the store with no projecting signs of any kind. In some centers, particularly strip centers with a canopy along the sidewalk, the tenants can have signs hanging underneath the canopy in front of their particular store. Usually the size of these signs is limited and the design of them is specified so that all of them can be uniform.

FORM OF LEASE

Usually the form of the lease will be determined by the office of the attorney that prepares it. In the case of chain stores, this will undoubtedly be the legal department of the particular chain store that is becoming a tenant. For local and smaller tenants, the lease will be prepared by the landlord's attorney.

Outline of Lease

Usually the lease begins with the major provisions such as the complete identification of the tenant, identification of the area leased, the amount of rent and the primary term. The other and more special provisions do not necessarily have to fall in any particular order. The order in which they appear will usually be a matter for the individual attorney drawing it to determine.

Attachments such as plot plans, or any photographs or building plans, should be attached to the lease as supplements or schedules. In the case of chain stores, the chain store company will determine how many copies it needs. In addition to the copies that the chain store needs, the landlord will, of course, need at least two, one for him to keep at his office and one for his attorney to keep in a locked file in the attorney's office. Usually a chain store will also furnish a short form of lease, a copy of which is to be recorded at the courthouse and which is notice to the public that certain premises are leased and controlled by the particular company involved.

POINTS TO KEEP IN MIND

- There are certain basic lease provisions that must be in all shopping center leases.
- There are other unusual provisions that apply primarily only to

shopping center leases and to the particular shopping center involved. There can be a great number of these.

- The basic provisions pertaining to the lease should be shown first, and then the other usual and special provisions can be put in order desired. There should be sufficient copies made, and one short form should be recorded at the county courthouse in the county in which the shopping center is located.

Chapter 18

Money-Making Shopping Center Contracts

Any contract between the owner of the property to be developed and the developer is, of necessity, a very complicated and usually lengthy contract. The same observation is true of any contract between a leasing agent and the developer or the leasing agent and the owner. Since it takes a long time to develop a shopping center, and since it is a major operation, the contract must be carefully drawn in order to protect both parties.

CONTRACT BETWEEN OWNER AND THE DEVELOPER

Before entering into any contract, both the developer and the owner should assure themselves that the project is feasible. Usually the experience and knowledge of the developer is the biggest factor in determining whether or not the location is suitable and whether or not a successful shopping center can be developed. At the same time, a statement of projected development and projected income to be derived from the development should be made. If a logical conservative projection provides sufficient income to satisfy the owner of the property and the developer's remuneration is sufficient for him, then a contract can be drawn and entered into.

Term of Contract

Length of term of the contract would be determined in large measure by a projected plan of development. If it is expected to develop the entire property at one time, the length of term can be shorter than would be the case where it is developed in parcels. In the event the entire property is to be developed and built all at once, the contract still should be several years in duration as it takes a long time to get the proper leases. Even after the leases are obtained and signed by everyone, there is a long time that lapses in building the necessary buildings and for the construction to be complete and with all of the tenants paying rent. Certainly there should be a minimum term of five years with a provision that, at the termination of five years, any leases already made, even though the building is not yet completed, would count as completion of the project in figuring the remuneration for the developer. This clause of the lease could not only cover leases completed, but not yet paying rent, but also leases which are under negotiation. Leases under negotiation could be definitely identified by naming the expected tenants with whom the negotiations are held.

In the event the property is to be developed in parcels, which is frequently the case in very large shopping centers, then the contract could cover a considerably longer time. One way of doing this is to divide the terms of the contract into sections with four to five years on parcel one, an additional three or four years on parcel two, etc. Usually there is a clause in this type of contract that, after the completion of each parcel, the contract can be cancelled for any valid reason by either the owner of the property or the developer. This cancellation would, of course, not affect any remuneration due the developer for work already done on the first parcel.

Duties of Each Party

The portion of the development work to be done by the owner and the portion to be done by the developer should be carefully set out. In the event that the owner is not taking an active part in the development of the center, the developer will have complete charge, and his duties will include everything from getting leases to completing the building of the center and operating it after it is built. This would be especially true where the developer is buying the land from the owner and would, of course, become the owner himself. Where the owner is taking a partial interest in the shopping center or is putting his land in as a part interest, the proportionate interest that he would have should be carefully set forth and, if he is to take an active interest, the part that he is to play should be carefully described.

Fees

Where the developer is developing a shopping center which would be owned by a corporation or the owner of the land, the developer's remuneration must be set forth. One way this could be done would be to give the developer a part interest in the center for his development work. Another would be a flat fee for building and completing the center. Another way of calculating what the developer would get out of the center would be a commission on the rentals paid for a period of fifteen or twenty years.

If it is a corporation that is building the center, the developer could receive a substantial part of the capital stock as his remuneration. There are many ways that this can be done, but whatever is done should be done carefully and set forth explicitly in the contract.

Termination of Contract

There are certain contingencies that might arise that should terminate the contract. If the developer is an individual and not a corporation, the contract would be terminated upon his death. In this event there should be some provision to include the developer's heirs in any fees that might develop when the center is completed and in operation. If some leases have been obtained prior to the developer's death, commission on these leases should still go to his estate. If the development has not proceeded far enough for there to be any actual leases, then the developer's heirs could be compensated for the amount of money that he spent on advertising and promotion and promotion materials.

Other causes of termination of the contract would be the failure of the shopping center to develop. If, as a result of not being able to get leases or financing, the center does not develop, the contract should be terminated by all parties.

The death of the owner would not cancel the contract, and it should be stated in the contract that in the event of the owner's death, the contract would continue with his heirs. Another contingency that should be covered is the possibility of the owner selling the land to someone else, which he could do before the development is completed. To protect the developer against this, there should be a clause that the contract goes with the land and would be binding on anyone who purchased it. Particularly because of this clause, a copy of the contract should be recorded at the courthouse in the county in which the shopping center is to be built. This is to give notice to any prospective purchasers of the land that the land has an encumbrance on it in the way of a development contract.

Expenses of Development

The type of organization set up to develop the center will determine who pays the expenses of developing and building. If it is a contract where the developer is doing all of the work, he would be responsible for all of the expenses. In the event of a partnership deal with the developer and owner, then it should be set out that expenses of the development would be paid out of partnership funds. The same reasoning would apply in the event of a corporation.

In the event that the developer is employed to do the developing on a flat fee or a lease commission basis and has no part in the ownership of the center, it should be specifically set forth in the contract as to just what expenses are the responsibility of the developer and which are the responsibility of the owners. Generally speaking, all of the expenses should be borne by the owner with the possible exception of advertising the center and travel expenses of the developer. Here again, it is necessary to have a clause in the lease so that the developer can be reimbursed for these items in the event that the owners decide not to develop the property or should sell it, or for any other reason the contract should be terminated.

Responsibility of the Developer

It should be set out in the contract, especially if the developer is merely employed by the owners of the property or the owners of the center when it is completed, that the developer is to pursue the development of the center in a businesslike manner. This is an attempt to protect the owners from seeing the property tied up fruitlessly for a long period of time with a developer who, either through the fact that he is too busy on other projects or for any reason is indifferent, does not devote sufficient time and attention to fulfilling his part of the contract. In order to protect the owner, there is frequently a clause in the contract to the effect that if no leases have definitely been obtained by the end of the first year, the contract can be cancelled at the option of the owners. A broad clause which states that the contract will be terminated if the developer does not proceed in a businesslike manner is very difficult to interpret and could lead to a long and complicated law suit.

One method of protecting the owner is a clause in the contract to the effect that the owner can cancel the contract any time he wants to after the first two years, but, in this event, he must reimburse the developer for all his expenses plus a fair compensation for the time spent. This may be in the form of commissions on leases that were completed during the developer's contract or in some other manner.

If Owner Is a Corporation

Usually the owner of the shopping center will be a corporation. This corporation can be formed by the developer or the owner of the land, and may include a part interest for either one or both of them, or it may be a corporation where the stockholders do not include either the owner or the developer. In any event, the type of contract with the corporation would be about the same. The important thing is to be sure that the officers of the corporation who sign the contract have the power to bind the corporation in this manner. It is usually best to have a meeting of the board of directors who would authorize signature of the contract with the developer.

There are advantages and disadvantages in having many stockholders in the company. Some developers feel that it is a good idea for the corporation to have as one of its principal stockholders a contractor or builder. The theory is that the contractor or builder, as a part owner of the property, would devote more attention to it and do a better job at a more reasonable cost. This does not always work out as intended because, due to the fact that he is a part owner, the contractor feels that he is due special consideration. It is also felt advantageous to have an attorney as part owner, as well as any local businessman who would add prestige to the center.

If there is a very strong local department store that would be a desirable tenant for the center, part interest in the corporation could be offered to the owners of the department store. This is sometimes done to the mutual advantage of everyone concerned.

Joint Enterprise

In the event that the owner of the shopping center is to be not a corporation, but a joint enterprise between several individuals, it is generally best to have as few individuals involved as possible. The ideal would be for one person to be the owner and financial backer of the project. If this is impossible the number should not exceed three or four, due to the difficulty of getting agreement from many owners.

Experience has shown that where there are many owners of a shopping center, each one will have his own ideas as to the architectural treatment, the landscaping and the tenants that should be in the center. If there are a great many of these people, it is sometimes difficult to reach agreement, and the development progresses slowly for this reason.

Statement of Financial Responsibility

Certainly the owners of the property would want to be assured that the developer has sufficient financial resources to promote the center successfully and bear any expenses necessary in doing so. Usually there is a clause in the contract that the developer is to furnish the owners a financial statement.

Even more important is the financial ability of the owners to finance the construction of the center after leases have been obtained. There should be a clause in the contract to the effect that the land is free and clear from all indebtedness or that the owners guarantee that they can clear it, and also a statement as to how much additional cash capital the owners can put into the venture. Certainly the owners should supply to the developer a financial statement to assure him of their ability to proceed with the shopping center and complete it as planned.

This clause should also state what happens in the event the owners are unable to complete financing and, for that reason, the center is not built. In this case, certainly the developer should be compensated for the expense and time that he has spent in the project. This could be done by a statement of expenses made by the developer and with a percentage, which would be definitely set out in the contract, of these expenses which would be paid to him as the fee for his services and the time and effort spent.

One of the most frustrating things for a developer is that, after getting a number of leases for a center arranged in such a way that the center would be a profitable one, to find that the owners, for financial or other reasons, cannot proceed with the construction of the center. If the developer is not protected against this contingency, he might find himself with two or three years' work and many thousands of dollars spent as expenses with nothing whatever to show for it.

CONTRACT WITH LEASING AGENT

Frequently the developer of the shopping center will be a different individual from the leasing agent. This is often true when the owners of the property will be owners of the shopping center and wish to develop it themselves. Usually they are not acquainted with real estate managers of various chains and do not know a great deal about how to go about getting leases. They will then appoint a leasing agent whose duty it is to obtain leases for them. This is mutually advantageous, as it gives the developers the services of a specialist in this field and if properly protected, it is a source of excellent earnings for the leasing agent. In fact for most real estate brokers, it is about the only way to get a continuous fixed income in the real estate brokerage business.

Before entering into a contract of this nature, each party should be certain of the other's ability to perform. This may involve an interchange of financial statements.

There should also be a feasibility study to determine in advance whether or not the location is a good one for a shopping center, and there should be some guidelines set up as to the amount of rentals that must be obtained in order to return a profit to the developer.

Terms

The contract must, of course, be an exclusive one. In cases where the developer has allowed a number of real estate agents to try to find tenants for him, there have been many complications. Sometimes it is hard to tell just which agent did bring any one certain prospect. For this reason the contract should be exclusive, with the agent having the only right to solicit leases.

The length of the contract should be at least five to ten years, as it takes a long time to get a complete set of shopping center leases.

Responsibilities of Each Party

The agent should commit himself to the extent that he will work in an effective manner to obtain leases, and the developer should commit himself to the extent that he agrees that he will build the center if enough leases have been obtained.

Fees

Usually fees to leasing agents are based on the amount of rents paid. Frequently these payments only concern the primary term of the lease, provided the lease is ten years or longer. This percentage will vary anywhere from 1 to 5 percent depending on the difficulty anticipated in getting leases. The usual figure is 2½ percent. From the broker's standpoint, it is an excellent way of receiving a consistent income over a period of years, as he can receive commissions on the leases in the shopping center each year for, in some cases, as long as twenty years. An important thing from a leasing agent's standpoint is that, in the event of his death or disability, any remaining commissions shall be paid to his estate.

Another important feature is some provision in the contract that, in the event the owner decides not to develop the property as a shopping center, the leasing agent can be reimbursed for the time and expense that he has already invested in the development.

Expenses

Usually the developer will bear all expenses of the shopping center except travel expenses and advertising of the agent. In some cases the developer bears advertising expenses and has to approve all advertisements before they are made.

Termination of Contract

The exclusive right to obtain leases may terminate in from three to five years. Of course any leases obtained during that period would bear full commissions and should be paid over the term called for, in many cases up to twenty years. This clause should also have a provision that at the time of termination, the broker shall be entitled to commissions at the regular prescribed rate on any leases that have been made or that are in process of negotiation at the time of the termination date.

The contract would be terminated automatically on the death of the agent, and there is usually a provision that in the event the agent, even though living, is not active in working for the center, it can be terminated at the option of the developer.

Lease Copies

It is a good idea for the leasing agent to be furnished a copy of each lease. In this way he can look through these leases to be sure that he is not seeking tenants that are prohibited due to restrictions in previous leases. The leases that are recorded at the courthouse should have a notation on the bottom of them that they are subject to a commission to the agent. The best way to do this is to have a rubber stamp made saying that this lease is subject to commission according to the contract with the developer.

POINTS TO KEEP IN MIND

- Contracts between owner and developer or leasing agent must be carefully prepared to protect both parties.
- The contract should cover a long term and should specify the duties of each party and the fees to be paid.
- In addition to the above, the contract should set forth how it is to be terminated, who bears which expenses of the development and the responsibility of both parties.
- It is important that each party receive a financial statement of the other so there can be no doubt as to their ability to proceed.

Index

Index

A

P

U

V

W

Z